THE MIND'S SIGNATURE!

RETHINKING OF LIFE'S PURPOSE

SURESH SHAIVA

Made with ♥ on the Notion Press Platform
www.notionpress.com

This book is dedicated to you. May it ignite your imagination and inspire you to explore the intricate workings of the human mind. May it encourage you to question the status quo, challenge assumptions, and seek the truth.

May you find within these pages a glimpse of the infinite possibilities that lie within each and every one of us, and may it remind you that we all have a unique "mind's signature" that is waiting to be uncovered and shared with the world.

This book is dedicated to my father Sri.Basavaraj, My Wife Smt Ramya Suresh Shaiva

Thank you for joining me on this journey of discovery.

Contents

Contents

Foreword

The Mind's Signature is a captivating exploration of the intricate and fascinating world of the human mind. Through this book, the author takes us on a journey of self-discovery, uncovering the unique "mind's signature" that defines who we are and how we interact with the world around us.

My approach to understanding the human mind is refreshingly insightful, offering a new perspective on the intricate and complex workings of our inner world. With each turn of the page, we are drawn deeper into the author's world, exploring topics ranging from neuroscience and psychology to philosophy and spirituality.

Through personal anecdotes, research, and thought-provoking insights, concise understanding of the human mind that will leave readers feeling informed, inspired, and empowered to embrace their unique potential.

The Mind's Signature is a must-read for anyone who seeks to understand themselves and the world around them. It is a powerful reminder that we all have the capacity to tap into our innate wisdom, unlock our unique potential, and make a positive impact on the world.

Regards
Suresh Shaiva

Preface

The Mind's Signature is a culmination of my lifelong fascination with the workings of the human mind. As , I have always been drawn to the complexities and mysteries that lie within our inner world. Through my personal experiences and academic pursuits, I have come to believe that we all have a unique "mind's signature" that defines who we are and how we engage with the world.

This book is an attempt to explore and understand the concept of the mind's signature. I draw on a range of disciplines, including neuroscience, psychology, philosophy, and spirituality, to provide a comprehensive understanding of the human mind. Through the pages of this book, I hope to offer readers a fresh and insightful perspective on the intricacies of our inner world.

Acknowledgements

Writing a book is a deeply personal and challenging endeavor, and I could not have completed this project without the help and support of many individuals. I would like to take a moment to express my gratitude to those who have made The Mind's Signature a reality.

First and foremost, I would like to thank my family and friends for their unwavering support and encouragement throughout this journey. Your love and belief in me have been a constant source of inspiration, and I am grateful for all the sacrifices you have made to allow me to pursue my dreams.

I am also deeply indebted to my colleagues, mentors, and professors, who have provided invaluable guidance, feedback, and support throughout the writing process. Your expertise and insights have greatly enriched the content of this book.

I would like to extend my sincere thanks to the staff and editors at Notion Press, who have helped me transform my vision into a reality. Your professionalism, expertise, and support have been crucial to the success of this project.

Finally, I would like to express my gratitude to the readers of this book. Your interest and curiosity in the workings of the human mind inspire me to continue exploring and sharing my insights. I hope that this book will be a valuable resource for anyone seeking to unlock the infinite possibilities of their own mind.

Thank you.
Suresh Shaiva

Prologue

The human mind is a mystery that has fascinated and perplexed us for centuries. From ancient philosophers to modern-day neuroscientists, we have sought to understand the complex workings of our inner world. In this book, I embark on a journey of self-discovery to explore the concept of the mind's signature.

The mind's signature is the unique pattern of thoughts, emotions, and behaviors that define who we are and how we engage with the world. It is the product of our genes, environment, experiences, and choices. Understanding the mind's signature is a crucial step towards unlocking our full potential and making a positive impact on the world.

Through this book, I draw on a range of disciplines, including neuroscience, psychology, philosophy, and spirituality, to provide a comprehensive understanding of the mind's signature. I share personal anecdotes and insights, as well as research and academic scholarship, to offer a fresh and insightful perspective on the complexities of our inner world.

My hope is that this book will be a source of inspiration and empowerment for anyone seeking to unlock their full potential and understand the unique qualities that make them who they are. I invite you to join me on this journey of self-discovery and exploration.

Suresh Shaiva

Free Consulataion

Since you bought this book, You will get 1-2-1 FREE consultation session for 30 Mins based on availability of slots

Savikalpa Holistic Center

Mobile 6364895551/9538735551

Youtube @savikalpaholisticcenter
Facebook Savikalpaholisticcenter
Website www.savikalpaholisticcenter.com

CHAPTER ONE

The Deed's Signature

The Power of Deeds -

In 2012, I was working at HDFC in the training department. One of my colleagues, Nanda, and I were close friends. However, Nanda had a negative attitude and constantly caused problems within the organization. Despite my attempts to discourage him, he continued with his negative behavior.

Eventually, I received an offer from SBI and decided to leave HDFC. Later on, a candidate who had previously worked at HDFC came for an interview at SBI. My manager asked me to give my feedback on the candidate, as he had received negative feedback from others. I was honest in my assessment and told the management that the candidate was talented but short-tempered and had caused problems in his previous job. Based on my feedback, the candidate was not hired.

Years later, I found myself feeling stagnant at SBI and applied for a job at Kotak. I made it through several rounds of interviews and was told that I would receive an offer letter soon. However, after resigning from SBI, I never heard back from Kotak. When I called the supervisor, I was told that negative feedback had been given about me. I was shocked, especially since the supervisor had previously praised me.

I reached out to a friend at Kotak and discovered that the person who gave the negative feedback was none other than Nanda.

Despite the fact that Nanda was not aware that I had given him negative feedback in the past, the universe had a way of balancing things out. This was a powerful lesson for me and showed me the impact of our actions, even when we do not intend to cause harm. It also taught me that we may never know the damage we inflict on others until it is done to us. This is the power of Karma.

What you sow: expect the same reap:

The idea that our thoughts and beliefs can shape our reality is not new, and has been a part of various philosophical and spiritual traditions for centuries. The concept of the subconscious mind and its role in shaping our lives is also well-established in psychology. It is believed that the subconscious mind operates outside of our conscious awareness and stores our past experiences, beliefs, and habits.

The concept of sowing and reaping, as described in the quote, refers to the idea that we will experience the consequences of our thoughts and actions. If we focus on positive and productive thoughts, we are more likely to attract positive experiences and circumstances into our lives. On the other hand, if we dwell on negative thoughts and beliefs, we are more likely to attract negative experiences.

The idea that everything in the universe is made up of energy and is interconnected is also not new. This idea is central to many spiritual and philosophical traditions and has been explored by scientists in the fields of physics and quantum mechanics. The concept of the universe as a vast, interconnected web of energy is known as non-dualism and suggests that everything is interconnected and part of a greater whole.

In conclusion, the idea that our thoughts and beliefs can shape our reality and that everything in the universe is interconnected is a powerful one that has been explored for centuries. By being mindful of our thoughts and beliefs and focusing on positive and productive ones, we can potentially attract more positive experiences into our lives and tap into the power of the universe.

To create good karma,

We must focus on our actions that are a result of our own volition. Volition, or our will, can be either good or bad, which in turn affects the outcome of our karma. The quality of our volition, or our mental impulse, is what determines the ethical nature of our actions. It lies at the intersection of our emotions and reason. A negative volition stems from negative attitudes and intentions, and to avoid bad karma, we must align our actions with positive attitudes and intentions.

To achieve this, we need to work on our attitudes and intentions first, keeping our thoughts and feelings pure. Our intentions drive our actions and can have significant consequences in our lives. By working on ourselves in the present, we can build a better future for ourselves.

Remember, what we do now will have an impact on the future, just as our past actions are affecting us in the present. We can still make positive changes, even if we have made mistakes in the past. For instance, if we choose to study better, we can still achieve our dream job or graduate in the course we love, even if it takes longer than we planned. By making a schedule and balancing our priorities, we can still be successful in our job. By exercising, we can still lead a healthy life.

However, to make lasting change, it is important that our efforts come from a deep compassion towards ourselves and others, and a good attitude and intention. Nothing is set in stone, and our past does not define us. What we do today can shape our present and future.

Where is Your Mind?

Your mind is constantly active, never truly going anywhere. Despite this, it is still here and present, always in one piece with your body and yourself. In order to live a fulfilling life, you must consider all three aspects together, not treating them separately. This is because the mind often tricks us into thinking that it is separate and roaming elsewhere, but in reality, it is always here.

The reason your mind is constantly racing and filled with endless thoughts is due to your attachment and identification with things that are not truly a part of you. To calm the mind, it is not a matter of control, but rather a matter of awareness. The first step towards this is recognizing and disconnecting from false identifications, such as your body, clothing, family, education, and religion.

Taking time for yourself, away from the chaos and noise of the mind, is crucial in this process. When you step back and disengage from the mind, it helps to disconnect from all false identifications. Remember, it is the mind that creates these false perceptions, so focus on simply being instead of getting caught up in thoughts. Trust that things will unfold in a way you never imagined, and let the mind simply be a tool for clarity and understanding.

Desire a conscious process

The common belief is that desire is the root of all suffering, but this is not entirely true. The source of suffering is unfulfilled desire, while fulfilled desire brings happiness. Many teachings encourage individuals to eliminate all desires, but this is not the solution. Desire is not a problem, but the way in which it is expressed can be. If desires are unconscious, they drive individuals to pursue them blindly and lead to an endless cycle of wanting more.

Desire is not separate from life, but rather a fundamental part of it. From the desire to move from one place to another, to the desire to read a book, desire is what drives us forward. It is the longing for something more, for growth and expansion. This longing for the infinite finds expression through desire, but if it remains unconscious, it creates problems.

Making desire a conscious process is key to avoiding suffering. By becoming aware of the social influences that drive desire, individuals can direct their desires towards fulfilling their own needs and goals. Desire is a powerful tool that can take individuals to great heights, even to reach the ultimate. It is important to bring awareness to the desiring process and make it a conscious part of one's life.

In conclusion, desire is not the source of suffering, but unfulfilled desire is. Making desire a conscious process can bring immense benefits and lead to personal growth and fulfillment. It is the responsibility of individuals to become conscious of their desires and use them as a tool for growth and self-discovery.

Describe the most important lesson you learned from this chapter and write 3 incidents from your own life

CHAPTER TWO

Inside Signature

Inside You!

Turn the management camera inside!

The quality of our lives, both internally and externally, is solely dependent on our ability to manage ourselves and our surroundings. Life is essentially a journey of management. When we are not able to maintain our bodies, minds, emotions, and social circumstances, chaos ensues. The main focus of society has become solely economic management, ignoring the other aspects of life. This has led to a world where happiness is difficult to find. People who have failed in life suffer, and those who have succeeded suffer their success. Happiness in life has become harder to come by as we age, and if our happiness is decreasing, it means we are poor managers of ourselves.

If you are unable to manage your own body, mind, emotions, and internal situations, managing external circumstances will always be accidental, not intentional. Being an accidental manager can lead to potential disasters, and an anxious and stressful life. Many believe that the nature of their job causes stress, but it is actually their own inability to manage themselves that leads to stress. In order to live a fulfilling life, we must strive to be managers of our own destiny, to ensure that we reach our full potential. Just as a top manager is responsible for the success of a company, every person must be responsible for their own success.

Education, job, money, and marriage are all sought after as ways to find happiness, but repeatedly they fail to deliver long-term joy and fulfillment. Seeking happiness through external means will only lead to disappointment. True happiness and fulfillment can only be found by properly managing oneself and rising to one's full potential. Throwing one's weight around is not true management, and can only lead to temporary happiness. It is time for people to understand that true happiness lies within, and can only be achieved through proper self-management.

What is really inside?

In a quaint village nestled in a valley, lived a man who radiated happiness and kindness wherever he went. His smile was infectious, and his words of encouragement left those he met feeling uplifted and rejuvenated. The people of the village looked up to him as a dear friend, always there to offer a helping hand.

One day, a curious villager decided to uncover the secret behind the man's unwavering positivity and generosity. They approached him on the street and asked, "Most people these days are self-centered and never satisfied, they rarely smile or show kindness like you do. What's your secret?"

The man replied with a warm smile, "When you find peace within yourself, you can spread that peace to those around you. By recognizing the spirit within yourself, you can see it in others, and it becomes natural to treat everyone with kindness and compassion.

The mind is like a programmed machine, controlled by habits and thoughts. To break free from this programming, you must learn to focus and control your thoughts. This takes effort and dedication to develop good habits, but it's worth it. The inner peace and happiness that lies within you will be revealed."

The villager sighed, "That sounds like a lot of work. It's not easy to control one's thoughts and emotions."

"Don't focus on the difficulty," the man advised, "Instead, try to find moments of stillness and peace within yourself. Watch your thoughts come and go, and stay in that peace. At first, these moments of peace may be brief, but with time, they will become longer. This peace is strength, power, kindness, and love.

In time, you will come to realize that you are one with the Universal Power, and this will allow you to act from a place of higher consciousness, not from a limited, ego-driven perspective."

The villager then asked, "Another thing I've noticed about you is that you seem unaffected by the environment around you. You always seem happy, even in the face of adversity. People treat you well, and never take advantage of your kindness."

The man replied, "Some people view kindness and goodness as a weakness, but that is far from the truth. Kindness and compassion come from inner strength, and this inner strength is what keeps people from imposing on you. When you are calm and in control, you can offer help without being taken advantage of.

Goodness and kindness do not equate to weakness. One can possess a good character and still be powerful and strong. When your mind is at peace, there is no room for anger or resentment, leading to happiness and contentment."

"Thank you for your wise words," the villager said, feeling grateful and content. They walked away, with a newfound understanding of the secrets to inner peace and happiness.

The moral of the story is that inner peace and happiness can be achieved by recognizing and making peace with one's own spirit and controlling one's thoughts and feelings. By doing so, one can naturally exhibit kindness, love, and inner strength, and not be swayed by external influences. Goodness does not equate to weakness, and inner calmness leads to happiness and contentment.

Mind can't live without leaving?

It is true that many people have become dependent on certain things in their lives, such as a morning cup of coffee, technology, or social media. These dependencies can create an emotional trap and drain our energy. However, it is possible to break these dependencies and become emotionally stronger. By starting small and changing our habits, such as not checking our phones or technology in the first hour of the day, we can create a more positive and empowered mindset. It is important to remember that we have the power to choose how we react to the world and to cultivate a high vibration state by focusing on our spiritual personality. Making simple changes in our lifestyles can help us to become emotionally independent and react to the world in a more positive and empowered way.

- Practice gratitude: Start each day by writing down at least three things you're grateful for. This will shift your focus away from what you lack and help you feel more positive.
- Engage in mindfulness practices: Whether it's meditation, yoga, or simply taking a few deep breaths, these activities can help you stay present and calm in the moment, which is key to emotional independence.
- Surround yourself with positive people: Seek out people who bring out the best in you and help you feel good about yourself. Limit your time with those who drain you or bring you down.
- Cultivate a growth mindset: Embrace challenges as opportunities to learn and grow, rather than obstacles that prevent you from reaching your goals. This mindset will help you bounce back from setbacks and build resilience.
- Take care of your physical health: Regular exercise, healthy eating, and adequate sleep are all critical components of emotional well-being. When you feel good physically, it's easier to feel good emotionally.
- Set boundaries: Know what you will and will not accept in your relationships and interactions with others. Having strong boundaries helps you maintain your emotional independence, even in challenging situations.

- Cultivate meaningful relationships: Make time for friends, family, and other important relationships in your life. Having supportive people around you can help you feel more grounded and connected.

By incorporating these habits into your daily routine, you can strengthen your emotional independence and resilience, and reduce your dependence on external factors for happiness and well-being.

Ignore the noise

It is important to find a balance between being informed and being consumed by the noise. We should be mindful of the sources of information we consume and be cautious of their motivations. It is also important to prioritize our own well-being and to focus on things that bring us joy and fulfillment, rather than constantly worrying about what others might think or say.

The Stoics also emphasized the importance of living in the present moment and not being too attached to things outside of our control. By focusing on what we can control, we can reduce our worry and increase our overall happiness and contentment. We can do this by setting goals and working towards them, as well as engaging in activities that bring us joy and fulfillment.

it is important to be mindful of the noise and opinions of others, but not to be controlled by them. By focusing on what we can control and prioritizing our own well-being, we can reduce our worry and increase our overall happiness and contentment.

Me Time

Making time for yourself and getting to know yourself is essential in order to have a fulfilling and meaningful life. By taking the time to reflect on your thoughts, feelings, and desires, you can better understand what you want in life and what your purpose is. Through the practice of concentration and mindfulness, you can focus your energy and attention on what is important to you, and in turn, find happiness as a by-product of living in alignment with your values and goals. It is important to prioritize self-care and self-reflection in order to live a fulfilling and purposeful life.

Serve yourself

It is important to prioritize self-care and to make the most of each day. By focusing on daily routines and activities that bring joy and satisfaction, we can reduce stress and anxiety and improve our overall well-being. It's a good idea to take a step back and assess what habits or activities bring us joy and satisfaction, and make an effort to incorporate those into our daily routine. Additionally, taking time to learn new skills or hobbies can not only help us deal with uncertainty but can also bring new opportunities and experiences. It is also crucial to acknowledge the impact of our environment and try to create a healthy and supportive one that encourages personal growth and well-being. By shifting our focus to the present and making the most of each day, we can live a more fulfilling life.

Summarize the most important points covered in this chapter, & how you plan applying these ideas in the future. Write 3 Take away

CHAPTER THREE

Beggining Hours Signature

The Begining Hours

The first hour of the morning is crucial for our emotional health. It sets the tone for the rest of the day and what we consume during this time will shape our thoughts and reactions. Our mind is like a blank slate in the morning, and whatever information we absorb during this time will be imprinted deeply in our subconscious mind. It is important to start the day with gratitude and focus on positive affirmations that align with our goals and aspirations.

Begin the morning with gratitude for everything you have in your life - God, your body, mind, people around you, and nature. This simple act of gratitude helps to tune your vibration frequency to a higher level of positivity and reduces the likelihood of negative thoughts and emotions throughout the day.

Create a personal set of affirmations that are related to your nature, personality, health, work, and relationships. Spend a few minutes in bed visualizing these affirmations and take them to a high vibration level. This helps to program your mind to respond in a positive way throughout the day when faced with challenging situations.

If you struggle with anger or irritation, create affirmations that promote peace, stability, and dignity in your responses. Visualize yourself responding calmly in various situations and allow the positive programming to become a part of your subconscious mind.

By starting the day with gratitude, affirmations, and visualization, we set ourselves up for a more fulfilling and productive day ahead.

Why it is important?

The first hour of the morning is crucial for our emotional well-being and can set the tone for the rest of our day. What we consume during this time can shape our thoughts, reactions, and overall outlook. Our mind is like a blank slate in the morning, making it an opportune time to imprint positive thoughts and emotions deep into our subconscious.

One effective way to begin the day is by practicing gratitude. By focusing on the things we are thankful for, such as our health, relationships, and even nature, we can elevate our vibrational frequency and reduce the likelihood of negative thoughts and emotions throughout the day. For example, you may wake up and feel grateful for a comfortable bed, a roof over your head, or a loving family. By acknowledging these blessings, you set a positive tone for the day ahead.

Another powerful tool is creating personal affirmations that align with our goals and aspirations. This involves developing positive statements related to our nature, personality, health, work, and relationships. Spend a few minutes in bed visualizing these affirmations and take them to a high vibration level. This helps to program your mind to respond positively when faced with challenging situations. For example, if you want to improve your health, you might repeat affirmations such as "I am healthy, strong, and energized" or "I am taking care of my body and mind every day." By consistently repeating these affirmations, you can rewire your subconscious mind and shift your beliefs and behaviors accordingly.

If you struggle with anger or irritation, you can create affirmations that promote peace, stability, and dignity in your responses. Visualize yourself responding calmly in various situations, and allow the positive programming to become a part of your subconscious mind. For example, you may repeat affirmations such as "I respond with calmness and grace in all situations" or "I choose to let go of anger and embrace peace." By doing so, you can retrain your mind to respond differently to triggers that may have previously caused negative reactions.

Research has shown that starting the day with gratitude and positive affirmations can have a significant impact on our emotional and physical well-being. For instance, a study published in the Journal of Happiness Studies found that individuals who practiced gratitude in the morning reported feeling more optimistic and satisfied with their lives. Similarly, a study published in the International Journal of Behavioral Medicine found that individuals who repeated positive affirmations in the morning experienced reduced stress and improved mood.

The beginning hours of our day are crucial for setting the tone for our emotional well-being. By starting the day with gratitude and positive affirmations, we can program our minds to respond positively to the challenges we may face throughout the day. This can lead to a more fulfilling and productive day, and ultimately, a more fulfilling life.

10 reasons why starting the day with gratitude and positive affirmations

- Sets a positive tone for the day: By beginning the day with gratitude and positive affirmations, we set a positive tone for the rest of the day.
- Reduces stress and anxiety: Practicing gratitude and positive affirmations can help reduce stress and anxiety by promoting positive thoughts and emotions.
- Increases happiness and satisfaction: Research has shown that individuals who practice gratitude and positive affirmations report feeling more optimistic and satisfied with their lives.

- Improves relationships: Gratitude and positive affirmations can improve relationships by fostering positive emotions, attitudes, and behaviors.
- Boosts self-esteem: Positive affirmations can help boost self-esteem by promoting positive self-talk and beliefs.
- Enhances resilience: Gratitude and positive affirmations can help enhance resilience by promoting a positive outlook and coping strategies.
- Increases productivity: By promoting positive emotions and attitudes, gratitude and positive affirmations can increase productivity and motivation.
- Promotes better health: Research has shown that practicing gratitude and positive affirmations can improve physical health by reducing stress and promoting better sleep.
- Encourages mindfulness: Practicing gratitude and positive affirmations encourages mindfulness and being present in the moment.
- Cultivates a positive mindset: By consistently practicing gratitude and positive affirmations, we can cultivate a more positive and optimistic mindset, leading to a more fulfilling and satisfying life.

Write 3 Things you do from tomorrow morning

CHAPTER FOUR

Self Improvement Signature

Self Improvement

1. Observe How People Treat Each Other: People's behavior often dictates how they are treated by others. Take note of how people are treated and how they behave. This can help you identify areas for improvement in your own behavior.

1. Observe Your Surroundings: Take note of how people behave in various situations around you. Observe people in your home, workplace, the grocery store, public transportation, and on the street. You can also learn a lot by watching interviews on TV.
2. Study People's Behavior: Watch how people speak, including their tone and volume, and pay attention to their reactions. Observe how people carry themselves when they walk or sit. You can learn a lot by analyzing their behavior.
3. Pay Attention to Vocal Cues: How people use their voices and react to others' voices can have a big impact on how you feel. Observe how you and others react to different tones and volumes of speech, including anger and calmness.
4. Identify What You Don't Like: If you see behavior you don't like, try to identify why it bothers you. Then, analyze your own

behavior to see if you exhibit the same negative traits.

5. Avoid Negative Behaviors: If you notice negative behavior in yourself, make a conscious effort to avoid it. Reaffirm to yourself that you will be aware of these behaviors and do your best to avoid them.

6. Use Visualization to Build Positive Habits: Imagine how you would like to behave and visualize it in your mind throughout the day. This can help build positive habits by sinking into your subconscious.

7. Emulate Positive Traits: When you see someone exhibiting traits you admire, try to act in a similar way. Visualize yourself behaving like them several times a day.

8. Visualize Frequently: Continuously think about and visualize the way you would like to behave and act.

9. Remind Yourself of Desired Changes: Constantly remind yourself of the changes you want to make and strive to act accordingly. Don't be discouraged if you don't see immediate results. Persevere with your efforts and you will begin to see positive changes in your life.

Blocks for Self Improvement

Having strong reasons is essential for achieving any goal. To build a better life, we need to use our reasons as building blocks. Personal, specific goals with clear deadlines and emotional attachment are more effective than vague, far-reaching ones. For example, wanting to fit into an old pair of jeans by a certain date is a better goal than just wanting to lose weight. Similarly, instead of just wanting more money, having a specific item to purchase by a certain date can be a more motivating goal. Using our own hopes and dreams as building blocks is the best way to ensure success in any life changes or improvements.

When it comes to setting goals and making positive changes in our lives, it's important to remember that our reasons for doing so are key to our success. The more personal and meaningful our reasons are, the more motivated and driven we will be to achieve our goals.

One way to identify our personal reasons for change is to ask ourselves the "why" behind our goals. For example, if our goal is to lose weight, we can ask ourselves why we want to do so. Is it to improve our health? Boost our self-confidence? Fit into a favorite outfit? By getting clear on our underlying motivations, we can tap into our deepest desires and harness that energy to fuel our progress.

Another important factor to consider is accountability. Sharing our goals with others, whether it's a friend, family member, or professional coach, can help us stay on track and committed to our objectives. In addition, breaking our goals down into smaller, more manageable steps can make them feel less daunting and more achievable.

Ultimately, the key to success in any endeavor is to stay focused on our reasons for doing it. By reminding ourselves of why we want to make a change, and staying committed to our goals, we can create a life that is fulfilling, purposeful, and meaningful to us.

Ready for change?

If you're reading this self-help article, you're already taking the first step towards a better you and a better world. Before diving into ways to initiate change, consider the wise words of Dr. Wayne Dyer: "If you change the way you look at things, the things you look at change." Instead of seeing negative traits as daunting obstacles, view them as minor hurdles that can be easily cleared. Focus on your determination, strength, and courage, and use them to pave a path towards success. By shifting your perspective to the positive, the negative will lose its grip on your life. Remember, you have everything you need to make the change you desire. Keep your focus on the good and the bad won't stand a chance.

Change is often difficult

Change is often difficult, even when we know what needs to change and why we want the change to occur. It is easy to fall back into old habits, even if they no longer serve us. However, setting small daily goals and working towards a larger goal can help create a new, positive path. For example, applying for an online degree program can help improve one's career or mental health. Buying a health-oriented book or focusing on positive affirmations can also help create an environment that encourages change. Success ultimately comes down to commitment, as committing to a single, reasonable purpose can help one achieve their goals. It is important to focus on the positive and battle FOR something rather than just against something, and committing fully to the desired change will ultimately lead to success.

All of us – every single one of us – have at least one change we need to make in our lives. We know full well what change needs to take place, and we certainly know WHY we want it to come about. The WHY may be more money, better health, better relationships, or better organization? Whatever the details, the change will be one that we know will add happiness and harmony to our lives.

Seems simple enough, right? What person in his or her right mind wouldn't do whatever needed to be done to bring more happiness into their lives?

Unfortunately, there's a reason I wrote "Seems simple enough" rather than just "Simple enough." Change is hard!

Funny, we always look at people around us and ask, "Why won't _____ just change?" or "Why can't _______ just give up smoking? He's not even trying!" Yet, when it comes to ourselves we fully recognize just how difficult it is to change habits – many of which are the habits of a lifetime. Trying to develop a new, better habit while trying to ditch an old one is like trying to create a new bike path, while ignoring the one that's already there.

It's so easy to steer back to familiar territory, isn't it... to follow the path we worked so long on creating. After all, the tires fit like a glove.

I wish there was an easy answer. If one existed, I'd be typing it out right now – happily letting my readers know the simple thing they needed to do to achieve all they wanted to achieve and to be all they wanted to be. I've given it a lot of thought and have done a great deal of reading and research (to say nothing of the trial and error approach I've had with my own habits!).

The best way to attain a positive change is to set a few small goals for you each day and work toward something larger. For example, if you're seeking to better your career or even improve your mental health, applying for school online is one way you can make an improvement to your life. It takes little effort to make the first step and apply. Just go online and see if any of the available degrees line up with some of your interests or passions. If you're accepted, you can even choose to take a small amount of classes based on what you're comfortable with.

You will have taken the first step in creating a new, positive path and the benefits will be more than worth the effort.

This holds true for those of us who are looking to improve our health. The first step may involve buying a new health-oriented book by a trusted author in the field of health. A great author can give you the information and tools you need to take your first step to a healthier life.

If you're looking to curb a nasty temper, negative attitude, foul mouth, or any other habit or trait you're tired of living with, I have one piece of advice... stop thinking about it! I'd better explain – I'm not saying to keep the habit, far from it. However, the more you focus on the negative, the deeper the groove becomes in your mind. If you keep on thinking, "I have got to get this temper under control," for example, you are simply creating a deeper groove in your mind that says, I HAVE A BAD TEMPER. Instead, focus on the positive, the flip-side.

Begin saying things like...

• "I am becoming so easy-going and even-tempered." • "Why am I such an even-tempered person?!" (experts say that, whatever the reason, putting positive affirmations into the form of questions is even more powerful) • "I stay.

How has your thinking or behavior changed as a result of reading this chapter?

CHAPTER FIVE

Point A to Point B
Signature

Point A to Point B

The journey from Point A to Point B is not always a straight line, but it's important to keep moving forward with determination and purpose. "Every step towards your goal is a step closer to success, never give up."

Having a strong will is essential to reach Point B. It's like a muscle that needs to be trained and developed through consistent effort. "The strength of your will determines the height of your reach."

It's important to always finish what you start, whether it's a small task or a major project. It builds a sense of accomplishment and sets the foundation for success in all areas of life. "Completing what you start is the cornerstone of greatness."

Balancing your life is key to achieving happiness and fulfillment. It's not about dividing your energy equally, but about directing it towards what truly matters most. "Balance is not about distributing your energy evenly, it's about directing it towards your priorities."

Incorporating this practice into every aspect of your life, from conversations to daily tasks, can bring great changes and lead to a more fulfilling life. "The power to change lies within the choices we make, in every moment."

Take control of your life, and make the conscious decision to see things through to the end. You'll be surprised by the results and how much you can accomplish. "Finish what you start, and start what you finish, that's the way to live a life with no regrets."

Completing a project is like climbing a mountain. When you start, you're full of excitement and energy, but as you get closer to the summit, the climb becomes more challenging. This is where will power comes in - it's like a muscle that you can build through persistence and determination. Just like how a climber needs strength and endurance to reach the top, developing will power will help you see things through to the end in every aspect of your life. It's important to bring this same sense of completion into your daily routine, like making sure your bed is neatly made before going to sleep, or putting away your toys after playtime. When you adopt the habit of finishing what you start, it will bring big changes to your life. The same goes for conversations - make sure to end them before moving on to the next task. A balanced life is like a beautiful symphony, where each note is played with equal emphasis and in harmony with the rest. Balance isn't just about dividing your time equally, but about directing your energy towards the things and people that truly matter. When you can find the right balance, your life will flow with harmony and purpose.

10 Tips Balance Life

- Prioritize your tasks: Identify your most important tasks and prioritize them based on their level of urgency and importance. This will help you manage your time more effectively and ensure that you focus on the tasks that matter the most.
- Create a schedule: Set aside specific times for work, personal time, and self-care. Having a structured schedule can help you manage your time more effectively and ensure that you allocate

enough time to all areas of your life.

- Set boundaries: Learn to say no to commitments that do not align with your priorities or values. Setting boundaries can help you manage your time and energy more effectively.
- Practice self-care: Make time for activities that help you relax and rejuvenate, such as exercise, meditation, or reading. Prioritizing self-care can help you reduce stress and improve your overall well-being.
- Delegate tasks: Learn to delegate tasks to others when possible. This can help you free up time and focus on the tasks that are most important to you.
- Limit distractions: Identify and minimize sources of distractions, such as social media or email notifications. This can help you stay focused and improve your productivity.
- Manage your workload: Be realistic about what you can accomplish in a day or week. Avoid taking on too much and manage your workload in a way that is sustainable and manageable.
- Set realistic goals: Set achievable goals that align with your priorities and values. This can help you stay motivated and focused.
- Practice gratitude: Take time to appreciate the good things in your life. Practicing gratitude can help you maintain a positive outlook and improve your overall well-being.
- Seek support: Reach out to friends, family, or professionals when you need help or support. Building a support system can help you manage stress and stay balanced.

Think about the examples or case studies presented in this chapter. How do they illustrate the concepts or ideas discussed, and how can you relate to

• 25 •

CHAPTER SIX

Change's Signature

Change starts with us

"Change Starts with Us" - this powerful phrase holds great truth and serves as a reminder that we have the power to shape our own lives and create the world around us. In every moment, we have the opportunity to choose the thoughts we think, the words we say, and the actions we take. These choices have the power to shape our lives and the lives of those around us.

For instance, imagine that you are unhappy with your job, feeling stuck and unfulfilled. Instead of resigning yourself to this situation, you can choose to take control and make changes in your life. Perhaps you start by researching new job opportunities, or taking online courses to improve your skills. You might also work on developing a growth mindset, and actively seeking out positive experiences and relationships. In doing so, you can take the first step towards a more fulfilling life.

Similarly, if you are unhappy with the state of the world, you can choose to make a difference by volunteering, supporting causes you believe in, or even just being kind to those around you. The small actions you take can ripple out and have a positive impact on the world.

This idea of "Change Starts with Us" is also embodied in the life of the Buddha. Before his enlightenment, he lived a life of luxury and privilege, but he was not satisfied. He set out on a journey of self-discovery, searching for the truth of existence and the end of suffering. He realized that change must start from within, and he dedicated himself to the practice of mindfulness and compassion. Through his efforts, he achieved enlightenment and became a source of guidance and inspiration for millions of people.

In conclusion, the phrase "Change Starts with Us" reminds us that we have the power to create the lives we want and the world we desire. Instead of resigning ourselves to fate or circumstance, we can choose to take control, make positive changes, and have a lasting impact on the world.

"The path to enlightenment is not an easy one, but it is a journey worth taking. Just like the Buddha, we too have the potential to awaken to our true nature and overcome suffering. The key is to be proactive and take control of our lives. It may seem like life is throwing challenges our way, but it's up to us to rise above them and work towards a better future. We can start by following the Eightfold Path - Right View, Right Resolution, Right Speech, Right Action, Right Livelihood, Right Effort, Right Mindfulness, and Right Concentration. These habits, if cultivated consistently, will help us transform ourselves and lead us towards a life of peace and happiness. The Buddha's life serves as an inspiration for all of us, reminding us that change starts with us and that we have the power to shape our own destiny. Let us strive to make progress each day, reading and researching more about the path to enlightenment, and supporting each other along the way."

"Pain is inevitable, suffering is your choice"

The phrase highlights the idea that while we may experience pain in our lives, whether it be physical or emotional, it is ultimately up to us how we choose to deal with it. The pain that we experience can be magnified in our minds, depending on how we choose to think about it. Many people find themselves stuck in a cycle of suffering, replaying past events and negative thoughts in their minds, causing themselves even more distress.

However, our perceptions play a big role in how we experience the world around us. If we start the day with the belief that the world is complicated and confusing, that is the lens through which we will see everything. On the other hand, if we approach the world with a positive attitude, we are more likely to have a better day. It is important to question whether the world is truly complicated, or if it's just our thinking that has become clouded.

We often blame the world for our pain and suffering, but the reality is that our thoughts and beliefs play a big role in how we experience life. It is all too easy to get caught up in the cycle of worrying and negativity, but we have the power to change that. By pausing and reflecting, we can identify the root causes of our distress and make a conscious effort to change our thinking.

It is also important to note that we have become addicted to feeling negative emotions. We are often searching for something to worry about, even digging up past experiences to create emotional turmoil. However, it is possible to break this cycle and find happiness and peace within ourselves. To do this, we must challenge our belief systems and understand that our emotions are not solely a result of external stimuli. By taking responsibility for our own emotions and choosing to react in a positive way, we can live a life free of suffering.

As a real-life example, consider a person who is going through a difficult breakup. While the initial pain of the breakup is inevitable, they have the choice to either dwell on their negative thoughts and suffer, or to focus on personal growth and find happiness in other areas of their life. Another example could be a person who experiences chronic pain. They may have the choice to focus on the pain and let it consume them, or to find ways to manage their pain and live a fulfilling life.

It is important to understand that our thoughts and emotions are not controlled by external circumstances, but by our own perception and interpretation of those circumstances. The way we choose to think about things can either amplify our suffering or lessen it. This is why two people can experience the same situation in different ways. One person may see it as a challenge and be motivated to overcome it, while another person may see it as an insurmountable obstacle and feel overwhelmed by it.

A powerful tool to shift our perspective and reduce our suffering is mindfulness. Mindfulness is the practice of bringing our attention to the present moment and observing our thoughts and emotions without judgment. This allows us to gain a new perspective on our experiences and understand that our thoughts and emotions are not permanent, but rather transitory. By acknowledging and accepting our feelings, instead of resisting them or trying to avoid them, we can release ourselves from their grip and reduce our suffering.

Real-life examples of this can be seen in individuals who have experienced trauma or loss, but have been able to find peace and happiness through mindfulness practices. By learning to accept their emotions and process them in a healthy way, they are able to move forward and find meaning in their lives.

It is also important to understand that change starts within. If we want to see a positive change in the world, we need to start by changing ourselves. By becoming more mindful and compassionate towards ourselves, we can cultivate inner peace and radiate that peace out into the world.

pain is an inevitable part of life, but suffering is a choice. By shifting our perspective and learning to accept and process our emotions in a healthy way, we can reduce our suffering and find happiness in the present moment.

As you reflect on the content of this chapter, think about how you can incorporate the 3 ideas

CHAPTER SEVEN

Mindfulness Signature

Mindfulness

Mindfulness is a mental state achieved by focusing one's awareness on the present moment, while calmly acknowledging and accepting one's feelings, thoughts, and bodily sensations. It helps to reduce anxiety, stress and worry, and increase happiness, well-being and peace of mind. In a world where we are constantly bombarded by stimuli, mindfulness allows us to slow down and focus on the present moment, instead of constantly worrying about the future or dwelling on the past. By practicing mindfulness, you can become more aware of your thoughts and emotions, and develop a greater sense of inner peace and control. This can help you to be more effective in your daily life and to handle stressful situations more effectively.

There are many ways to practice mindfulness, including meditation, deep breathing exercises, yoga, tai chi, and mindful walking. You can also integrate mindfulness into your daily routine by being present in the moment while you perform daily activities like eating, showering or commuting. You can start with small steps, such as taking 5-10 minutes each day to practice mindfulness and gradually increase the time as you become more comfortable with the practice. Additionally, incorporating mindfulness into your family routine, by doing mindful activities together, can help to reduce stress and increase feelings of closeness and connection within the family. Remember, the goal of mindfulness is not to escape from the challenges and problems of life, but to face them with clarity, equanimity and compassion.

21 Advantages of Mindfulness

1. Reduced Stress: Mindfulness has been shown to significantly reduce stress levels, which can lower the risk of depression and anxiety.
2. Improved Emotional Regulation: Mindfulness can help you better regulate your emotions and respond to negative thoughts and feelings with greater ease.
3. Increased Self-Awareness: Regular mindfulness practice can help you gain a deeper understanding of yourself, including your thoughts, feelings, and motivations.
4. Better Focus and Concentration: Mindfulness can help you focus better and avoid distractions, leading to improved productivity and performance.
5. Improved Relationships: Mindfulness can help you communicate more effectively and respond to others with compassion and empathy, leading to stronger relationships.
6. Increased Resilience: Mindfulness can help you develop a greater ability to cope with stress and adversity, making you more resilient.
7. Reduced Chronic Pain: Mindfulness has been shown to be effective in reducing chronic pain and discomfort.
8. Improved Sleep: Mindfulness can help you fall asleep faster and enjoy more restful sleep, leading to better physical and mental health.
9. Improved Physical Health: Mindfulness can help you improve your overall physical health by reducing stress levels, boosting the immune system, and reducing inflammation.

10. Decreased Blood Pressure: Mindfulness has been shown to help lower blood pressure, reducing the risk of heart disease and stroke.
11. Decreased Symptoms of Depression: Mindfulness has been shown to reduce symptoms of depression and improve overall mood.
12. Increased Happiness: Regular mindfulness practice has been shown to increase feelings of happiness and well-being.
13. Improved Cognitive Function: Mindfulness can help improve cognitive function and reduce age-related declines in memory and attention.
14. Better Decisions: Mindfulness can help you make better decisions by allowing you to think more clearly and respond to challenges with greater ease.
15. Increased Creativity: Mindfulness can help increase creativity by allowing you to think outside the box and approach problems from different perspectives.
16. Increased Compassion: Mindfulness can help you develop a greater sense of compassion for others, leading to improved relationships and greater happiness.
17. Improved Body Image: Mindfulness can help you develop a healthier relationship with your body and improve your self-esteem and confidence.
18. Increased Self-Acceptance: Mindfulness can help you accept and embrace your thoughts, feelings, and experiences, leading to greater self-awareness and self-compassion.
19. Improved Relationships with Food: Mindfulness can help you develop a healthier relationship with food, leading to better eating habits and weight management.
20. Increased Energy: Mindfulness can help increase energy levels and reduce fatigue, allowing you to tackle challenges with greater ease.
21. Improved Mental Health: Mindfulness can help improve overall mental health and reduce the risk of depression, anxiety, and stress-related disorders.

Inward changes

Inward changes can have a profound impact on one's life and growth. As Prime Minister Narendra Modi has often discussed, it is crucial to be aware of the instruments of our experience in order to fully understand our existence. The five sensory organs - sight, hearing, smell, taste, and touch - are the only ways that we can know that we are here in the present moment. Without these sensory organs, our experience of life would be completely different.

PM Modi has emphasized the importance of being conscious and fully involved with the people and world around us. Belonging to a community or belief system can provide a sense of security, but it can also lead to sleepwalking through life. In order to truly live, one must be fully awake and conscious of their surroundings.

PM Modi has also highlighted that we do not know much about the world and our existence. We may think we understand things, but in reality, our knowledge is limited. For example, we do not fully understand a blade of grass, a single atom, or a single cell in our body. This realization can lead to a constant seeking of knowledge and understanding, which is intrinsic to human intelligence.

However, people often seek comfort in belief systems, rather than seeking knowledge for its own sake. PM Modi has noted that belief systems can hold us back from truly seeking and exploring the world around us. It is important to be aware of our beliefs and to not pretend to know things that we do not know. By freeing ourselves from these belief systems, we can tap into our innate human intelligence and embark on a journey of self-discovery and growth.

Take some time to consider the key messages of this chapter and how you can use them to enhance your personal and professional development.

CHAPTER EIGHT

Mystery Signature

Mind Mystery

I have heard this from one of my mentor.

In the past, two Monks lived in adjacent caves near a village. The Monks were known for their deep meditation and peaceful teachings, which attracted many visitors. Despite their popularity, the Monks remained quiet and reserved, not wanting to discuss the source of a peculiar golden light that sometimes illuminated one of their caves.

The villagers were fascinated by the light, but couldn't agree on its origin. Some believed the Monk in the illuminated cave possessed supernatural powers, making him seem more advanced. However, when a well-known sage visited the village, the villagers asked for clarification on the mystery of the light.

The sage advised the villagers to pay attention to their inner self, and not to external phenomena, when in the presence of a teacher. He then explained that when one works intensively on their spiritual path, they can produce various phenomena such as lights, sounds, or visions. These phenomena are not supernatural, but rather the result of a concentrated mind. Not all minds produce these things, and it has nothing to do with one being more advanced than the other.

The sage also explained that some of the people who produce these lights may be aware of them, while others may not, and that it depends on their psychic sensitivity. The villagers were grateful to the sage for solving the mystery that had been puzzling them for so long. In the end, the sage emphasized that the most important thing is to listen to the teachings of a teacher and be aware of the impact on one's inner self.

The moral of the story is that one should focus on the inner self and the teachings of a spiritual teacher, rather than external phenomena, in order to gain a deeper understanding of spirituality and reach a state of peace and happiness. The sage emphasizes that the most important thing is to be aware of the impact that a teacher's words have on one's inner self and to listen to those teachings. The phenomenon of the light in the cave is a secondary matter and should not be the focus of one's spiritual journey.

Mind vibration power. Your thoughts becomes your vibration, your vibration becomes your reality

The story of the yogi and his disciple highlights the concept of mind vibration power. The idea is that your thoughts create your vibration, and your vibration influences your reality.

One day, the yogi and his disciple arrived in a big city with no money but in need of food and shelter. The disciple assumed they would have to beg for food and sleep in the park, but the yogi had a different idea.

The yogi told his disciple about the power of thoughts and how intensely focusing on something can make it happen. He demonstrated this by closing his eyes and meditating with full concentration. After a few minutes, they walked to a hotel where the manager approached them and offered them food and a place to stay in exchange for work in the kitchen.

The disciple was shocked and asked the yogi how he made this happen. The yogi explained that the power of thoughts works through concentration, visualization with detail, faith in the power of thoughts, and projecting mental and emotional energy into the mental scene created in one's mind.

The yogi warned that one should be careful with what they think, as a concentrated thought can have a strong influence on the environment. The disciple realized the importance of sharpening his concentration to use this power effectively.

The moral of the story is that the power of thoughts can be harnessed to create a positive reality. With concentration, visualization, faith, and mental and emotional energy, one can turn their thoughts into reality.

Silence the inner Noise

It is important to find a balance between being informed and being consumed by the noise. We should be mindful of the sources of information we consume and be cautious of their motivations. It is also important to prioritize our own well-being and to focus on things that bring us joy and fulfillment, rather than constantly worrying about what others might think or say.

The Stoics also emphasized the importance of living in the present moment and not being too attached to things outside of our control. By focusing on what we can control, we can reduce our worry and increase our overall happiness and contentment. We can do this by setting goals and working towards them, as well as engaging in activities that bring us joy and fulfillment.

It's important to be mindful of the noise and opinions of others, but not to be controlled by them. By focusing on what we can control and prioritizing our own well-being, we can reduce our worry and increase our overall happiness and contentment.

it's important to understand that the noise created by other people's opinions and judgments can have a profound effect on our mental and emotional well-being. This is why it's so important to learn how to ignore it and focus on what's truly important in our lives. This requires a certain level of self-awareness and introspection, as we must first understand what truly matters to us, what our goals and priorities are, and then work to stay focused on these things despite the noise around us.

One way to ignore the noise is to cultivate a strong sense of self-confidence and self-esteem. When we are confident in ourselves, we are less likely to be swayed by other people's opinions and judgments, and we are better able to make decisions that are in line with our own values and goals. To build self-confidence, it's helpful to focus on our strengths, accomplishments, and positive traits, and to work on developing a growth mindset, where we see challenges as opportunities for growth and improvement.

Another way to ignore the noise is to surround ourselves with positive and supportive people who encourage and uplift us, rather than those who bring negativity and criticism into our lives. This can be done by seeking out positive relationships, and by actively seeking out new friends who share our values and interests. It's also helpful to limit our exposure to negative people, whether that means spending less time with them, or simply unfollowing them on social media.

Finally, it's important to engage in activities that help us stay centered and focused, such as meditation, mindfulness, or simply taking time to relax and recharge. This can help us to stay calm and centered in the face of stress and negativity, and to remain focused on what truly matters to us, even when the noise around us is at its loudest.

By taking these steps to ignore the noise, we can reclaim control of our thoughts, feelings, and decisions, and live more fulfilling, happy, and meaningful lives.

Mind loitering and losing focus

Mind loitering and losing focus is a common problem in today's fast-paced world. People often think that the mind is going somewhere, but the truth is, it's always here, present in the present moment. The mind is always thinking about something, but it doesn't physically go anywhere. Similarly, your body doesn't go anywhere, and neither do you. They are all one composition and you cannot handle them separately. To bring balance and clarity to your life, you need to take care of both the mind and the body together.

Many people struggle with controlling their thoughts and find it difficult to quiet their mind. This is because they have become too identified with things that they are not. When you are identified with things that do not truly define you, such as your body, clothes, job, education, etc., the mind becomes a never-ending cycle of thoughts and distractions.

A recent example of this can be seen in the rise of technology addiction, where people are so identified with their phones and social media that they can't seem to put them down, even for a moment. Another example can be seen in people who are so focused on their careers that they forget to take care of their health and relationships.

Meditation and mindfulness are often recommended as ways to calm the mind, but if you're still identified with things that you are not, these practices may not work. The key is to create a little distance from the mind and disengage from your identities. This can be done by taking time for yourself, focusing on the present moment, and being aware of your thoughts and feelings without judgment.

Just like a noisy mind doesn't matter once you disengage from it, things will start to happen in your life that you may not have even imagined. By letting go of your identifications, you can bring more clarity and focus to your life and enjoy the present moment.

Consider the practical applications of what you've learned in this chapter and how you can use these insights to improve your own life.

CHAPTER NINE

Attachment Signature

Minds attachment to detachment

A lotus leaf grows inside the water. But it never sticks the water. Our life too should be like this. Be with the family; do not get attached to it.

This analogy of the lotus leaf is a powerful reminder to live our lives with a sense of detachment, while still being fully present and engaged in our relationships. When we become too attached to the people and things in our lives, we open ourselves up to suffering and disappointment. Attachment can lead us to cling to the past, fear the future, and become overly attached to the present moment. This can cause us to miss out on the joy and richness of life that is all around us.

On the other hand, when we practice detachment, we are free to embrace each moment for what it is, without being burdened by our fears and worries. We can be fully present with our loved ones, experiencing their joys and sorrows with them, but not becoming overly attached to their every move. This allows us to enjoy the beauty of life, free from the stress and anxiety that often accompany attachment.

In essence, living like the lotus leaf means cultivating a balanced relationship with the world around us, where we can be fully engaged and connected, while also being mindful and detached. This is the path to true happiness and peace, and it is a lesson that we can all learn from the lotus leaf.

However, detachment does not mean being cold or unfeeling. It means letting go of our attachment to material things, emotions, and people. When we are attached, we become emotionally invested in a situation or person and it becomes difficult for us to let go. This can lead to feelings of anger, resentment, and disappointment. Detachment, on the other hand, allows us to be present in the moment without getting caught up in our emotions. It helps us to maintain a calm and clear state of mind, even in the face of challenging situations.

The practice of detachment requires us to be mindful and aware of our thoughts, emotions, and actions. By focusing on the present moment, we can learn to let go of our attachment and not get caught up in the drama of life. This can bring a sense of peace and inner happiness, even in the face of life's challenges. When we are detached, we can approach every situation with clarity and compassion. We can make decisions based on what is best for everyone involved, rather than just what makes us happy.

Detachment is a powerful tool that can help us live a more fulfilling and joyous life. It requires us to be mindful and aware of our thoughts, emotions, and actions, and to let go of our attachment to material things, emotions, and people. By practicing detachment, we can maintain a calm and clear state of mind, even in the face of life's challenges, and live a life filled with peace and happiness.

How it is possible?

One day, a wise sage was sitting by a river, watching the water flow by. A young man approached him and asked for his advice. The young man was feeling overwhelmed by his emotions and was seeking a way to escape the turmoil he was experiencing. The sage listened attentively to the young man and then told him a story.

Once upon a time, there was a tree that stood by a river. The tree had many branches, each one representing an emotion or attachment the tree had. The tree was so weighed down by these branches that it was difficult for the tree to stand tall and proud. However, one day, the tree learned the secret of detachment. The tree realized that it could still have its branches, but it did not have to be controlled by them.

The young man listened intently to the sage's story and asked for further guidance. The sage explained that detachment in spirituality is about letting go of our attachment to material things, people, and emotions. It's about realizing that everything is temporary and that we are not defined by what we have or what we feel. Instead, we are defined by our spirit, which is eternal and unchanging.

The young man was fascinated by the sage's words and asked if there was a way he could start practicing detachment in his own life. The sage nodded and told him to start by observing his thoughts and emotions without judgment. When a thought or emotion arises, simply acknowledge it and let it pass, like a leaf floating down the river.

The young man took the sage's advice to heart and began to practice detachment in his daily life. He found that he was able to let go of his attachments and was no longer burdened by his emotions. He was free to live in the present moment and enjoy the beauty of life.

Detachment in spirituality is about releasing our hold on things that we cannot control and embracing the present moment. By doing so, we can find peace and happiness in our lives. Like the tree that learned to stand tall and proud, we too can learn to let go of our attachments and find peace in the flow of life.

Understanding in deeper sense

I heard this from my mentor

A story about detachment is about two monks who were traveling from one village to another. They came across a large puddle filled with mud, and a young woman was standing at the edge, unsure of what to do. The first monk asked if she needed help crossing the puddle and offered to carry her on his back. He carried her to the other side and continued on the journey with the other monk. After hours of walking in silence, the second monk couldn't take it any longer and asked how the first monk could carry a woman, as monks were not allowed to touch women. The first monk smiled and replied that he had already left the woman at the puddle, but it seemed that the second monk was still carrying her.

This story highlights the importance of detachment in spirituality. The first monk carried out his good deed without attachment, keeping his mind calm and focused on the journey ahead. Meanwhile, the second monk couldn't let go of the incident and kept dwelling on it, wasting his time and energy.

Detachment, in spirituality, means being a detached observer and protecting oneself from the energy of a situation and people. The concept of detachment may not be a comfortable one for many of us, as we associate attachment with love and beauty. However, in spirituality, detachment means releasing attachment to material things and focusing on the present moment, which can lead to a greater sense of peace and calmness.

Detachment comes in handy

This is where detachment comes in handy. Detachment means letting go of the attachment to the situation or the person. It does not mean cutting off all relationships, but rather taking a step back and not getting involved in the negative energy. When you detach yourself, you create space between you and the situation, and you can see things more clearly. This way, you protect your own peace of mind and well-being.

One simple technique to practice detachment is to focus on your breath. When you feel stressed or upset, take a moment to close your eyes and take a deep breath. Exhale slowly, and imagine that you are letting go of the attachment to the situation. Repeat this process as many times as necessary. You can also imagine a bright light surrounding you, protecting you from the negativity. This light acts as a barrier, and helps you to stay calm and centered.

Another technique is to practice mindfulness. This means being present in the moment, and focusing on your thoughts, emotions and sensations. When you are mindful, you are not lost in the past or worrying about the future. Instead, you are fully engaged in the present moment. This helps you to let go of the attachment to the situation or person, and to see things with a clear mind. Detachment is an important aspect of self-care and personal growth. It helps you to protect your own peace of mind, and to avoid getting entangled in negative situations and relationships. By practicing detachment, you can cultivate inner peace, and live a happier and more fulfilling life.

Detachment from negative thoughts

Detachment from negative thoughts is a crucial aspect of mental and emotional well-being. Negative thoughts can consume our mind, cloud our judgment and lead to a life of unhappiness and stress. The past can haunt us and cause us to dwell on negative experiences, leading to a cycle of negative thinking. It is important to break this cycle and focus on the present moment.

One effective way to do this is through emotional detachment. This means separating yourself from your thoughts and emotions, and not letting them control you. This allows you to observe your thoughts objectively, rather than being consumed by them. When you are able to distance yourself from your thoughts, you can choose to focus on positive experiences and create a happier life.

By controlling your attention, you can choose to focus on the present moment and let go of past experiences. This can bring a sense of peace, happiness and freedom into your life. Additionally, focusing on the present moment also helps to create a better future, as it ensures that we are doing our best in each moment.

To practice emotional detachment, start by paying attention to your inner conversations and thoughts. Notice which ones are negative and try to let them go. Replace them with positive affirmations and focus on the present moment. It may take time and practice, but with persistence and determination, you can learn to let go of negative thoughts and experience the freedom and happiness that comes with emotional detachment.

Detachment does not mean cutting people

Detachment can be beneficial for you as it allows you to maintain emotional and mental stability, keep negative thoughts and emotions at bay, and avoid being affected by other people's moods and problems. When you are detached, you are in control of your thoughts, emotions and reactions. You are not allowing anyone to manipulate you or affect you negatively.

Detaching yourself from people who make you feel stressed can be difficult, but it is necessary for your well-being. You need to evaluate the relationships in your life and determine which ones are positively contributing to your growth and happiness, and which ones are causing distress. If you find that someone is causing you stress, try to reduce the amount of time you spend with them or limit the level of attachment you have with them.

It is also important to remember that detachment does not mean cutting people out of your life completely. It is about creating healthy boundaries and not letting others have an adverse impact on your emotional and mental well-being. It is about finding a balance in your relationships and taking care of your own well-being.

Escape certain people or situations?

What if you cannot escape certain people or situations? Sometimes, the people closest to you can be the ones who disrupt your inner peace. This is where emotional detachment comes in.

Emotional detachment is not about giving up on people or things, or breaking communication and becoming indifferent. It's about protecting your mental and emotional well-being by remaining calm and composed in stressful situations. It's about not allowing negative thoughts and emotions to impact your state of mind or behavior.

You can still maintain relationships, work towards your goals, and do the things you love while practicing emotional detachment. It means distancing yourself from the negative emotions and thoughts that others may project, while still being loving and considerate.

Attachment and detachment apply to not only people, but also to possessions and things. Enjoy what you have, but if you lose something or it breaks, it's important to stay calm and move on. This mindset can help save you from heartache, pain, and unhappiness.

Mentally and emotionally detaching yourself from anything that creates stress, distress, and unhappiness will bring freedom, lightness, and happiness into your life. Attachment can make you feel weak, helpless, and worried, but detachment will make you feel strong, confident, invulnerable, and happy.

Letting go

"Letting go involves releasing attachments to things that cause you pain or discomfort. It involves letting go of your attachment to things that don't matter to you or that make you unhappy. This means detaching yourself from negative, pointless, or harmful thoughts and emotions. By doing this, you free yourself from emotional burdens and stop taking things too personally.

Letting go is a process of letting go of persistent, unpleasant thoughts and feelings. While this may seem challenging, with practice, it becomes easier. Just as you wouldn't hold on to old, torn, or useless clothing, you shouldn't hold on to negative thoughts, bad habits, unhealthy lifestyles, or even people who cause you suffering or unhappiness.

At times, it may be necessary to let them go and even forget about them. Letting go is like pulling up the anchor of your ship so that you can start sailing. You cannot sail when the anchor is holding you back. In the same way, you need to let go of the things that are holding you back in life."

Attachment causes pain why?

Because you expect!

Attachment can bring pain because we have expectations. It's important to understand the difference between attachment and detachment. Physical attachment is like being physically connected to another person, like conjoined twins. But emotional attachment is when our mind is connected to someone else's mind and our emotions are dependent on them. When someone we love is in pain, we naturally feel their pain too. But instead of experiencing the same pain as them, we can be detached but still present to support them. This is what they need, not someone who is just as affected as they are.

Meditation and spirituality help us take care of our own mind, so our thoughts and feelings aren't dependent on others and situations. When we're stable and strong, we can support others even during a crisis. It's important for each family to have at least one person who is emotionally stable to be able to support the others. People need emotional support, not just physical support. And we can provide that by first taking care of ourselves and giving others the emotional strength to heal themselves.

Being kind to others means giving them emotional strength, not just advice or sympathy. When someone is going through a tough time, they need more than just words of encouragement. They need emotional support to fill the vacuum inside them and heal. That's our responsibility when we say we want to be kind to others. By shifting our focus from attachment to detachment, we can heal and empower those around us.

What have you learned from this chapter and how can you apply it in your life? Write 3 points

CHAPTER TEN

The Unknown Signature

Unknown Terrain To Known Terrain.

"Every new challenge is just history repeating itself in a different form" - this age-old truth couldn't be more relevant than in the year 2019, when the world was grappling with the uncertainty surrounding the Covid-19 pandemic. Cities and countries were shutting down, and we all found ourselves watching the headlines with a sense of unease, wondering what would happen next. The fear of losing jobs, money, and even loved ones was palpable, and it was all too easy to fall into a state of worry and panic.

But if we take a step back and look at the bigger picture, we'll see that the same patterns of life repeat themselves time and time again, just with different characters and formats. From the Black Death to SARS to the Spanish Flu, the world has faced similar crises before, and it will likely face them again. Worry is a natural part of life - it's our brain's way of trying to handle problems and keep us safe. But when it becomes persistent and uncontrollable, it can take a heavy toll on our emotional and physical well-being.

We need to understand that whatever we're worrying about, it's likely happened before and will happen again. What seems new and scary today will soon become old and familiar. We're adaptable creatures with a unique capacity to change and evolve with the ever-changing patterns of life. So instead of worrying too much, let's try to keep our calm and have faith in our ability to overcome any challenge that comes our way.

"The only constant in life is change, embrace it" - we may not know what the future holds, but one thing is for sure, things will change. And that's not necessarily a bad thing. Change brings new opportunities and growth, it helps us adapt and evolve. So instead of resisting change, let's embrace it with open arms.

"Don't let your worries weigh you down, they're just a part of the journey" - it's easy to get bogged down by worries and anxieties, but they're just a natural part of life's journey. Instead of letting them consume us, let's see them as stepping stones to our growth and evolution. Let's use them to become stronger, more resilient, and more capable of handling whatever life throws our way.

"The Power of Experience and Perception in Shaping Our Lives"

Our experiences shape who we are and how we perceive the world around us. Our five senses collect information from the environment, which our brain processes and organizes into patterns. These patterns are then stored as memories and shape our beliefs and perceptions. In fact, by the time we reach 35 years old, 95% of our thoughts, feelings, and behaviors are unconscious habits and reactions that are deeply ingrained into our neural circuitry.

For example, in the Mahabharata, the character Arjuna must overcome his beliefs and perceptions about war and his own worth as a warrior to fulfill his destiny. Similarly, in real life, we may hold beliefs about relationships, spirituality, or money that are based on past experiences, but may limit our possibilities and decision-making in the present.

In order to change our beliefs and perceptions, we must have a decision with such strong intention and energy that it surpasses the hardwired programs in our brain and body. This can happen when we have a transcendent experience that reorganizes the circuitry in our brain and sends a new emotional signal to the body. This is the moment when we become liberated from the past.

However, our thoughts and emotions can also have a physical impact on our bodies. When we think about something positive, such as a cup of coffee or a new puppy, our brain begins to produce the exact chemicals in anticipation of the event, preparing our body for the reward. On the other hand, when we think about negative events, such as a co-worker we dislike or pain, our body may also prepare itself for that experience.

Therefore, it's important to be mindful of our thoughts and emotions, and to work towards creating positive experiences that can break the cycle of negative beliefs and perceptions.

Reaching To Next Terrain

Life is full of unknown terrain. We all face new and unfamiliar situations at some point in our lives. Whether it's starting a new job, moving to a new city, or facing a personal crisis, these situations can be challenging and overwhelming. However, by understanding and learning from our experiences, we can transform unknown terrain into known terrain.

The process of transforming unknown terrain into known terrain starts with self-awareness. We need to understand our thoughts, emotions, and behaviors in response to new situations. For example, if we are starting a new job, we may feel anxious and uncertain about our ability to succeed. By acknowledging and understanding these feelings, we can begin to develop coping strategies to manage our anxiety and build our confidence.

One real-life example of this is the story of J.K. Rowling, the author of the Harry Potter series. After her divorce and the death of her mother, she found herself in an unknown terrain where she was unemployed, broke, and raising a child on her own. Instead of giving up, she channeled her emotions into writing a book, which became the first Harry Potter novel. By understanding and learning from her personal struggles, she was able to transform unknown terrain into known terrain and become one of the most successful authors of all time.

Another example is the story of Arunima Sinha, the first female amputee to climb Mount Everest. After losing her leg in a train accident, she faced a new and unfamiliar terrain where she had to learn to navigate life with a disability. Instead of giving up, she set herself a goal of climbing the world's highest mountain and dedicated herself to rigorous training. By understanding and learning from her experience, she was able to transform unknown terrain into known terrain and achieve her dream.

In both of these examples, the individuals were able to transform unknown terrain into known terrain by understanding and learning from their experiences. By acknowledging their emotions and developing coping strategies, they were able to build resilience and achieve their goals. This is a valuable lesson for all of us - that even in the face of the unknown, we can learn and grow, and ultimately transform our lives for the better.

Life is full of unknown terrain, but by understanding and learning from our experiences, we can transform it into known terrain. Self-awareness, coping strategies, resilience, and goal-setting are all essential tools in this process. By applying these tools, we can overcome challenges, achieve our goals, and transform our lives.

Summarize the key takeaways from this chapter and how you plan to implement them.

CHAPTER ELEVEN

History Signature

Everything is just history repeating

"Every new challenge is just history repeating itself in a different form" - this age-old truth couldn't be more relevant than in the year 2019, when the world was grappling with the uncertainty surrounding the Covid-19 pandemic. Cities and countries were shutting down, and we all found ourselves watching the headlines with a sense of unease, wondering what would happen next. The fear of losing jobs, money, and even loved ones was palpable, and it was all too easy to fall into a state of worry and panic.

But if we take a step back and look at the bigger picture, we'll see that the same patterns of life repeat themselves time and time again, just with different characters and formats. From the Black Death to SARS to the Spanish Flu, the world has faced similar crises before, and it will likely face them again. Worry is a natural part of life - it's our brain's way of trying to handle problems and keep us safe. But when it becomes persistent and uncontrollable, it can take a heavy toll on our emotional and physical well-being.

We need to understand that whatever we're worrying about, it's likely happened before and will happen again. What seems new and scary today will soon become old and familiar. We're adaptable creatures with a unique capacity to change and evolve with the ever-changing patterns of life. So instead of worrying too much, let's try to keep our calm and have faith in our ability to overcome any challenge that comes our way.

"The only constant in life is change, embrace it" - we may not know what the future holds, but one thing is for sure, things will change. And that's not necessarily a bad thing. Change brings new opportunities and growth, it helps us adapt and evolve. So instead of resisting change, let's embrace it with open arms.

"Don't let your worries weigh you down, they're just a part of the journey" - it's easy to get bogged down by worries and anxieties, but they're just a natural part of life's journey. Instead of letting them consume us, let's see them as stepping stones to our growth and evolution. Let's use them to become stronger, more resilient, and more capable of handling whatever life throws our way.

This is a pattern

Financial Crises: Throughout history, financial crises have occurred time and again, with similar underlying causes such as speculation, overleveraging, and inadequate regulatory oversight. For instance, the 2008 financial crisis was caused by the collapse of the housing bubble, which is similar to the collapse of the dot-com bubble in the early 2000s and the stock market crash of 1929.

Political Instability: Many countries have experienced political instability due to factors such as corruption, economic inequality, and social unrest. For example, the Arab Spring protests that occurred in the early 2010s in Tunisia, Egypt, and other countries were sparked by grievances that have been present for decades, including high unemployment, authoritarian rule, and lack of political freedoms. Similarly, the ongoing protests in Belarus over the disputed re-election of President Alexander Lukashenko in 2020 echo protests that occurred in the same country in 2006 and 2010.

Environmental Disasters: Environmental disasters such as oil spills, chemical leaks, and nuclear accidents have occurred repeatedly throughout history. For example, the Deepwater Horizon oil spill in 2010 was reminiscent of the Exxon Valdez spill in 1989, and both disasters had devastating impacts on the environment and local communities.

Wars and Conflicts: The causes and dynamics of wars and conflicts have been studied extensively by historians and political scientists, and many have observed patterns in the reasons and ways in which conflicts occur. For example, the rivalry between India and Pakistan over the disputed territory of Kashmir has led to multiple wars and skirmishes over the past few decades, with tensions remaining high despite occasional peace negotiations.

Overall, while history may not repeat itself in exactly the same way, there are certainly patterns and lessons to be learned from past events that can help us better understand and navigate the challenges of the present and future.

Now that you've finished this chapter, how has your understanding of the topic changed, and what actions will you take to implement this newfound know

CHAPTER TWELVE

Habit Signature

Effects of habit

Let's take the example of Arjuna from the Hindu epic, the Mahabharata, to understand the concept of habit formation. In the story, Arjuna is depicted as a great warrior who acquires his skills through repetition and consistent practice. He demonstrates how habit formation can be seen as a result of repetitive unconscious thoughts, behaviors, and emotions.

Just like Arjuna, we all have habits that we have acquired over time through repetition. Our habits are so ingrained in us that our bodies often know how to perform them better than our minds. For instance, when we wake up in the morning, our minds immediately start thinking about our problems and past experiences. These memories are connected to emotions and the moment we recall them, we suddenly feel unhappy, sad, or in pain. This is because our thoughts and feelings create our state of being. If we continue to live in the past and recall negative memories, we are more likely to experience a predictable future.

Moreover, our daily routines, such as checking our phones, social media, and going through a series of familiar behaviors, can also become habits that we follow without much thought. This can lead to a loss of free will as we become programmed to follow the same patterns.

To break free from this cycle, we need to get beyond our analytical minds and practice techniques such as meditation to change our brainwaves and slow them down. This will allow us to enter the operating system and make important changes to our habits. Often, people wait for a crisis, trauma, or loss to prompt them to change, but it's important to remember that change can happen at any time.

However, change can also be uncomfortable as our minds react based on past experiences. For example, if we have a fearful thought, we may feel anxious. This is why it's crucial to be aware of our thoughts and feelings and to make a conscious effort to feed our subconscious with positive thoughts and emotions.

In conclusion, Arjuna's story highlights the importance of repetition and consistent practice in developing habits and the impact of our thoughts and emotions on our state of being. By becoming more conscious and aware of our actions, we can break free from negative patterns and create a wonderful life.

Then what is it?

Habits are a repetitive set of automatic actions, thoughts, and emotions that are developed over time through repetition. They are performed so often that your body knows how to do them without you having to consciously think about them. In the morning, people often begin by thinking about their problems, which are actually circuits or memories in the brain that are linked to specific times, places, and people. These memories also come with emotions, which are the result of past experiences. When people think about their problems, they often feel unhappy, sad, or pain.

It is said that "how you think and how you feel creates your state of being." In the morning, people start the day in the past and this familiar past becomes a predictable future. Our feelings have become the means of thinking and we tend to keep creating the same life. People then check their phones, social media, news, and go through their daily routine, which becomes a programmed cycle. This routine takes away their free will and makes it difficult to change. Meditation can help break this cycle by changing brainwaves and allowing for important changes to be made.

People often wait for a crisis, trauma, disease, or loss to change, but now more and more people are waking up. The stronger the emotional reaction to an experience, the more it will be remembered as a long-term memory. People often think they cannot control their emotional reactions, but if they allow themselves time to process these emotions, they can change their response. Most people spend 70% of their life in survival mode and stress, anticipating the worst based on past experiences and limiting their potential. They become addicted to the rush of emotions and use problems in their life to reinforce their limitations.

Changing habits can be difficult because it requires making different choices, which can be uncomfortable. If you have a fearful thought, you will feel anxiety. Your mind always reacts based on previous experiences. It is important to be aware of what you are doing and make conscious choices that create a fulfilling life. Nourish your subconscious with positive thoughts and establish a good relationship with it.

15 Tips To Tune Good Habits

1. Start small: This point emphasizes the importance of starting with small habits to avoid becoming overwhelmed or discouraged. For example, instead of trying to establish a daily exercise routine, start with a five-minute stretch in the morning. Starting small allows you to build momentum and gain confidence, making it easier to tackle more significant habits

over time.

2. Be specific: When forming a habit, it's essential to be specific about what you want to accomplish and when you plan to do it. For example, if you want to start reading more, specify the time and duration you will read. By being specific, you can set achievable goals and measure your progress.

3. Make a plan: A plan is a crucial part of forming a habit as it allows you to establish a routine and create a sense of structure. When making a plan, consider the best time of day to execute the habit, how long you will devote to it, and any resources you will need. By making a plan, you will have a roadmap to follow, which can be helpful in staying on track.

4. Track your progress: Tracking your progress is an essential component of forming a habit. When tracking progress, you can see how much progress you've made and what areas may need improvement. It's also a good motivator because you can see the progress you've made, which can encourage you to keep going.

5. Get an accountability partner: Having someone hold you accountable is an excellent way to stay on track when forming a new habit. This person can provide motivation, guidance, and support, making it easier to stick to the habit. They can also offer encouragement and help you overcome any obstacles that may arise.

6. Reward yourself: Rewards are a great way to motivate yourself and maintain momentum when forming a habit. A reward can be anything from a small treat to a special outing, as long as it is something that motivates and excites you. Rewards can also create a sense of accomplishment and help keep you motivated.

7. Stay positive: A positive mindset is crucial when forming a habit. Instead of focusing on the effort required, focus on the benefits of the habit. For example, if you're trying to establish a regular exercise routine, focus on the increased energy and mood-boosting benefits rather than the effort required to exercise.

8. Be patient: Forming a new habit takes time, and it's essential to be patient with yourself during the process. It's common

to experience setbacks or struggle with maintaining the habit, but it's important to remember that progress takes time. With patience and perseverance, you can establish a successful habit.

9. Focus on one habit at a time: It's best to focus on one habit at a time to avoid feeling overwhelmed or spread too thin. Once you've established one habit successfully, you can move on to the next one. Focusing on one habit also allows you to devote your full attention to the habit and increases your chances of success.

10. Make it a part of your identity: When forming a habit, it's important to think of yourself as someone who has that habit, not just someone trying to establish it. By adopting the habit as part of your identity, it becomes easier to maintain, and you're more likely to stay committed to it.

11. Find motivation: Finding motivation for forming a habit is crucial, as it can help keep you committed and focused. This can be accomplished by identifying the benefits of the habit or setting specific goals that the habit will help you achieve. Motivation can also come from seeking inspiration from others who have successfully formed the habit.

12. Surround yourself with support: Surrounding yourself with supportive individuals can be helpful when forming a habit. This can

13. include joining a support group or online community, seeking out friends or family members who have similar goals, or even hiring a coach or mentor who can provide guidance and accountability.

14. Stick to a consistent routine: Consistency is key when forming a habit. Creating a routine that you can stick to, whether it's daily, weekly, or monthly, can help make the habit feel automatic and ingrained in your lifestyle.

15. Practice self-care: Practicing self-care is important when forming a new habit. This can include getting enough sleep, eating a healthy diet, and taking time to relax and destress. Practicing self-care can help you stay energized and motivated

to maintain the habit.

16. Don't give up: The final point is perhaps the most important. Forming a new habit can be challenging, and setbacks are inevitable. However, it's crucial not to give up. Instead, focus on the progress you've made so far and continue to work towards your goal. With persistence and dedication, you can successfully establish a new habit and enjoy the benefits that come with it.

Think about the main points discussed in this chapter and consider how you can integrate them into your daily routine. Write 3 Points

CHAPTER THIRTEEN

Belief Signature

When you believe!

An experiment conducted by researchers at Harvard Medical School, a group of hotel cleaners were told that the work they do on a daily basis is enough to meet the Surgeon General's recommendations for an active lifestyle. They were given a brief presentation and some basic information about physical activity, but no additional resources or instructions. A month later, the cleaners showed significant improvements in blood pressure, body mass index, and other health markers, even though they had not changed anything about their actual work routines. The only difference was that they believed their work was a form of exercise.

In another study, researchers found that students who were told they had a genetic predisposition for being "good at" a particular skill (in this case, math) outperformed their peers in math tests. The catch was that the researchers had randomly assigned the "math gene" label, so there was no actual genetic basis for the supposed ability. The students who believed they had the gene worked harder and had more confidence, leading to better results.

These experiments, along with many others, suggest that our beliefs and expectations can have a powerful effect on our actions and outcomes. When we believe we can succeed, we are more likely to take the necessary steps to achieve our goals. When we believe we are capable of change, we are more likely to make positive changes in our lives. And when we believe that what we are doing is important and meaningful, we are more likely to give it our best effort.

The placebo effect

The placebo effect is a phenomenon where a person's condition improves because they believe a treatment will help, even if the treatment is fake. It's often used in clinical trials to determine the effectiveness of new drugs. For example, if a group of people are given a drug and another group are given a placebo (a fake pill), and both groups show similar levels of improvement, it suggests that the drug is not effective.

While the placebo effect is often associated with deception and quackery, it's important to recognize that placebo improvements are still real improvements. For example, if an athlete is given a sugar pill and told it's a powerful steroid, they may still experience increased strength and endurance. This doesn't mean that the sugar pill was actually a steroid, but it does mean that the athlete's belief in the effectiveness of the treatment had a real, measurable impact on their performance.

The placebo effect is a complex and multi-faceted phenomenon that is not fully understood by scientists. However, there are a few theories that attempt to explain how it works. One theory is that the placebo effect is mediated by the release of endogenous opioids, which are naturally occurring pain-relieving chemicals in the brain. When a person expects a treatment to be effective, their brain may release endogenous opioids, which can produce real improvements in pain, mood, and other symptoms.

Another theory is that the placebo effect is mediated by classical conditioning, which is the process by which a neutral stimulus (like a sugar pill) becomes associated with a specific outcome (like pain relief) through repeated pairing. In this case, a person may come to associate the act of taking a pill with the expectation of feeling better, even if the pill itself has no active ingredients.

The placebo effect is not just limited to pills and other medical treatments. It can also occur in other contexts, such as in education, where a student's belief in their own abilities can influence their academic performance. For example, if a student is told that they are a gifted writer and are given positive feedback on their work, they may be more likely to excel in writing assignments, even if they don't have any inherent talent in that area.

The placebo effect is a reminder of the power of belief and expectation in shaping our experiences and outcomes. While it's important to be skeptical of false claims and to rely on evidence-based treatments, it's also important to recognize the role that our beliefs and expectations play in our lives. By harnessing the power of the placebo effect, we can potentially enhance our own health, performance, and well-being.

My Own Student experiment

The power of the placebo effect can often be seen in real-life situations, such as in the story of one of my students. This student suffered from frequent headaches and had become addicted to taking headache tablets as a way to manage the pain. However, after attending one of my classes on the power of the mind, she began to see the potential of the placebo effect to help her manage her headaches.

One day, when she felt a headache coming on, she decided to try an experiment. Instead of reaching for her usual headache tablet, she took out some polo chocolates and held them in her palms. She began to say to herself, "This is the headache tablet. It cures my headache." She repeated this statement several times and then ate the chocolates.

To her surprise, the headache disappeared within a few minutes. She was amazed by the power of her own belief and expectation in this situation. From that day on, she continued to use the placebo effect to manage her headaches, often using simple techniques like visualization and positive affirmations to create a sense of belief in the treatment she was using.

This story highlights the potential of the placebo effect to improve our lives, even in situations where traditional medical treatments may not be available or effective. It also underscores the importance of understanding the role that our beliefs and expectations play in shaping our experiences and outcomes. By harnessing the power of the mind, we can potentially tap into the placebo effect to improve our health, performance, and well-being.

It Works or Does not work in our hands

Believing that something works can be a powerful tool to tap into our untapped potential. This was a lesson I learned from my own experience. I had always been an average performer, never quite reaching my full potential. But one day, I stumbled upon the power of the placebo effect and how it could help me change my mindset.

I began to believe that I was capable of more than just average performance. With this new mindset, I found that I was actively seeking out all the reasons I would succeed, rather than focusing on why I might fail. My mind, body, and heart were all in sync, rowing in the same direction. It was like a switch had been flipped, and suddenly I was performing at a level I never thought was possible.

Of course, this kind of change doesn't happen overnight. It takes time and effort to balance psychology and performance. But the placebo effect showed me that I had untapped potential inside me just waiting to come out. And when I began to believe that I was capable of more, I found the courage and conviction to go after my goals with renewed vigor.

I began to approach my work with a newfound sense of purpose and focus, looking for ways to improve my performance and achieve my goals. And with every success, my belief in my own potential grew stronger. I found that the more I believed in myself, the more I was able to accomplish.

Looking back on my journey, I can't help but wonder what kind of results I might have achieved if I had believed in myself from the beginning. But I don't dwell on the past, I focus on the future and the potential that lies within me. With the power of the placebo effect and the belief in my own potential, I know that anything is possible.

The Repeated Bout Effect

Have you ever experienced the soreness that comes after returning to exercise after a break? It can be tough to get back into the swing of things, but it's the post-workout soreness that is really brutal. I know this firsthand, as someone who is passionate about strength training and always looking for ways to improve my performance. For example, after taking a few weeks off from squatting, it can be painful to sit in a chair or climb stairs later in the week. But here's the counterintuitive solution that I've found to work best: squat again.

I know it sounds crazy, but doing some light reps of squats is often the quickest way to recover from the soreness. I usually start with three sets of ten bodyweight squats. The first few reps are uncomfortable, but then my muscles limber up and I feel significantly better by the end of it. So why does this work? If squatting caused the pain, then why would more squatting resolve it? It's a concept called the Repeated Bout Effect, which is applicable to much more than just exercise.

The Repeated Bout Effect is a phenomenon where our body adapts to a repeated stimulus over time. When we first engage in a new activity, our body is not used to the stress and strain of that activity, so we experience soreness and fatigue. However, if we continue to perform that activity over time, our body adapts and becomes more efficient at performing it. As a result, we experience less soreness and fatigue over time. In other words, the more we do something, the better our body becomes at handling it.

This concept applies not just to strength training, but to any skill or activity that we want to improve at. For example, if you're learning a new language, practicing consistently over time is the key to success. The more you practice, the more your brain adapts to the language and becomes more efficient at processing it. Similarly, if you're trying to improve your writing, the more you write, the more your brain adapts to the process and becomes more efficient at generating ideas and structuring sentences.

This is the essence of deliberate practice, which is the intentional and focused effort to improve a skill or activity. Deliberate practice involves breaking down a skill into its component parts, practicing those parts individually, and then putting them back together to perform the skill as a whole. It requires focus, discipline, and a willingness to push through discomfort and failure in order to improve.

One of the best examples of deliberate practice in action is the training regimen of elite athletes. They spend countless hours practicing specific skills and movements in order to improve their performance. For example, a basketball player might spend hours practicing their jump shot or dribbling skills. A swimmer might spend hours practicing their stroke technique. These athletes push themselves to the limit in order to improve their performance and achieve their goals.

"The Repeated Bout Effect" and deliberate practice are powerful tools for self-improvement. Whether you're trying to improve your strength, learn a new skill, or achieve a goal, the key is to practice consistently over time. This may require pushing through discomfort and failure, but the reward is a stronger, more capable version of yourself. So the next time you're feeling sore after a workout, don't be afraid to squat again. Your body will thank you for it in the long run.

What did you learn from this chapter, and how will you apply it in your life? Write 3 Points

CHAPTER FOURTEEN

Suffring Signature

Why we suffer?

Suffering is a complex and multi-faceted phenomenon that can result from various factors. Some of these factors include:

- Wanting more than enough: As you mentioned, many people suffer because they feel inadequate or unhappy with what they have, and instead focus on wanting things that don't necessarily add value to their lives. The media can contribute to this by perpetuating the idea that happiness is tied to material possessions and wealth.

- Attachment to the ungraspable: Attaching ourselves deeply to temporary things, such as material possessions, can lead to suffering when we lose them or they become damaged. It's important to understand that these things are not a part of our true self, and instead to focus on identifying with the divine intelligence, which is a permanent source of wealth and happiness.

- Not realizing the source of creation within us: Many people believe that they are only physical beings, but it's important to understand that we are also spiritual beings with the divine intelligence within us. Recognizing this can help us overcome challenges and reduce suffering by giving us a sense of inner power and wisdom.

- Comparing ourselves to others: Comparing ourselves to others can bring stress and suffering because there will always be someone who is better or has more than us. It's important to focus on our own progress and avoid comparing ourselves to others, as this only leads to feelings of inadequacy.

It's important to keep in mind that everyone experiences suffering in their own way, and there is no single solution or approach that works for everyone. However, by understanding these factors and working to minimize their impact on our lives, we can take steps towards reducing suffering and finding a sense of inner peace and happiness.

Are you riding the horse? Or horse is riding you? In context – Are you controlling the mind or is your mind controlling you?

Yes, it is true that the thoughts and ideas we encounter can greatly impact our thoughts, emotions, and behavior. However, it is important to remember that we have the ability to choose what thoughts and ideas we allow to occupy our minds. This requires self-awareness and intentional effort to regulate our thoughts and reactions. With practice, we can develop the ability to recognize when our mind is being influenced by external factors and choose to direct our focus towards more positive and productive thoughts. This is the essence of mindfulness and mental control, where we become the rider of our horse, instead of the horse riding us. It takes effort and practice, but it is possible to take control of our mind and thoughts.

10Tips To Handle Suffering

1. Understand the nature of suffering: Suffering is a natural part of life and an opportunity for growth. By understanding that suffering is a part of the human experience, we can accept it as an opportunity to learn and develop our spiritual selves.

2. Practice self-awareness: Through practices such as meditation, prayer, and journaling, we can become more self-aware and develop an understanding of our emotions and thought patterns. This can help us identify the root causes of our suffering and work towards healing.

3. Cultivate compassion: Compassion for ourselves and others can help alleviate suffering. By extending kindness and understanding to ourselves and those around us, we can develop empathy and connect with others on a deeper level.

4. Focus on gratitude: By focusing on what we are grateful for, we can shift our attention away from our suffering and towards the positive aspects of our lives. Gratitude can help us cultivate a sense of joy and contentment.

5. Connect with a higher power: For those who believe in a higher power, connecting with that power through prayer or meditation can provide comfort and support during times of suffering.

6. Practice forgiveness: Forgiveness can be a powerful tool in overcoming suffering. By releasing grudges and resentments, we can move forward with a greater sense of peace and freedom.

7. Seek support from others: We do not have to go through suffering alone. Seeking support from friends, family, or a professional counselor can provide a safe space for us to share our struggles and receive guidance.

8. Practice acceptance: Accepting our circumstances, even if we do not like them, can help us find peace and move forward. By accepting what we cannot change, we can focus on what we can control and work towards positive change.

9. Develop resilience: Resilience is the ability to bounce back from difficult situations. By developing resilience through practices such as exercise, healthy eating, and positive self-talk, we can better handle challenging situations and overcome suffering.

10. Embrace impermanence: Nothing in life is permanent, including our suffering. By recognizing the impermanence of our struggles, we can cultivate a greater sense of hope and optimism for the future.

Take a moment to reflect on the key takeaways from this chapter and how they relate to your own experiences. Write here

CHAPTER FIFTEEN

Subconscious mind Signature

The Inner Treasure! Your Subconscious mind

The power of the subconscious mind is an incredible force that often goes overlooked in our daily lives. Our subconscious mind is responsible for storing and processing information that we are not always consciously aware of, and it has a profound influence on our thoughts, feelings, and behaviors.

Many experts in the field of psychology and personal development believe that the subconscious mind is the key to unlocking our true potential and achieving our goals in life. By harnessing the power of the subconscious mind, we can overcome our fears, limiting beliefs, and negative thought patterns that hold us back from living the life we truly desire.

One of the most powerful ways to tap into the power of the subconscious mind is through visualization. When we visualize our goals and dreams, we create a mental image that our subconscious mind can use to manifest our desires into reality. This is because the subconscious mind cannot tell the difference between a real experience and one that is imagined. By visualizing our goals as if they have already been achieved, we create a powerful force that attracts the people, circumstances, and resources we need to make them a reality.

Another way to tap into the power of the subconscious mind is through positive affirmations. Affirmations are positive statements that we repeat to ourselves on a regular basis to create new thought patterns and beliefs. By repeating affirmations such as "I am confident and capable" or "I am worthy of love and success," we reprogram our subconscious mind to believe these statements as truth. This, in turn, can lead to positive changes in our lives and a greater sense of self-esteem and confidence.

The subconscious mind is also responsible for our habits and automatic behaviors. By consciously changing our habits and thought patterns, we can reprogram our subconscious mind to support our goals and desires. For example, if we want to become more physically fit, we can create new habits such as exercising regularly or eating a healthy diet. Over time, these new habits become automatic, and our subconscious mind begins to support our efforts to become healthier and more fit.

In order to tap into the power of the subconscious mind, it's important to quiet the conscious mind and allow the subconscious to take over. This can be done through meditation, hypnosis, or other relaxation techniques. By quieting the conscious mind, we open ourselves up to the messages and insights that the subconscious mind has to offer.

In conclusion, the power of the subconscious mind is an incredible force that can help us achieve our goals and overcome our fears and limiting beliefs. By harnessing the power of visualization, positive affirmations, and conscious habit change, we can reprogram our subconscious mind to support our desires and create the life we truly want. With practice and persistence, we can tap into the power of the subconscious mind and unlock our full potential as human beings.

Why subconscious is so powerful?

The subconscious mind is a powerful force that influences our thoughts, emotions, behaviors, and ultimately our lives. It operates outside of our conscious awareness, yet it plays a critical role in shaping our experiences and perceptions of the world. In this article, we will explore why the subconscious mind is so powerful and how we can harness its potential to achieve our goals and live more fulfilling lives.

The subconscious mind is responsible for many of our automatic and habitual behaviors, such as breathing, blinking, and walking. It also stores our memories, beliefs, and emotions, and influences our decision-making processes. Our subconscious mind is constantly working in the background, processing information, and generating automatic responses based on our past experiences and conditioning.

One of the key reasons why the subconscious mind is so powerful is its ability to process information at an incredible speed. Unlike the conscious mind, which can only process a limited amount of information at a time, the subconscious mind can process millions of bits of information simultaneously. This allows it to quickly analyze patterns, identify threats, and make snap decisions based on our past experiences.

Another reason why the subconscious mind is so powerful is its connection to our emotions. Our emotions are an essential part of our human experience, and they are generated by our subconscious mind in response to external stimuli. Our subconscious mind can quickly analyze a situation and generate an emotional response based on our past experiences and conditioning. This is why we sometimes feel fear, anxiety, or sadness without even knowing why.

Our subconscious mind is also responsible for creating and reinforcing our beliefs. Beliefs are the mental constructs that shape our perceptions of reality and influence our thoughts, emotions, and behaviors. Many of our beliefs are formed in childhood, and they can be difficult to change because they are deeply ingrained in our subconscious mind. This is why some people may have limiting beliefs that hold them back from achieving their goals or living their best lives.

The power of the subconscious mind lies in its ability to influence our conscious thoughts and behaviors. Our subconscious mind is like a silent partner that is constantly working behind the scenes to shape our experiences and perceptions of the world. It can influence our thoughts and emotions, which in turn can affect our behavior and decision-making processes.

If we want to harness the power of our subconscious mind, we need to learn how to communicate with it effectively. The subconscious mind communicates in symbols and images, rather than language, which is why visualization and other forms of imagery are so powerful. By using techniques such as visualization, meditation, and self-hypnosis, we can communicate with our subconscious mind and reprogram our beliefs and habits.

One of the most powerful ways to harness the power of our subconscious mind is through affirmations. Affirmations are positive statements that we repeat to ourselves to reinforce positive beliefs and behaviors. By repeating affirmations, we can train our subconscious mind to focus on positive outcomes and to generate positive emotions that support our goals.

Another way to harness the power of the subconscious mind is through the use of positive self-talk. Our inner dialogue is a constant stream of thoughts and beliefs that influence our emotions and behavior. By practicing positive self-talk, we can reprogram our subconscious mind to focus on positive outcomes and to generate positive emotions that support our goals.

In conclusion, the subconscious mind is a powerful force that influences our thoughts, emotions, and behaviors. Its ability to process information quickly, generate emotions, and shape our beliefs makes it a critical component of our human experience. By learning how to communicate with our subconscious mind and reprogram our beliefs and habits, we can harness its power to achieve our goals and live more fulfilling lives.

10 top ways to reach subconscious mind

1. Visualization: Visualize yourself achieving your goals in detail. See it as if it has already happened. Your subconscious mind will work to bring your vision into reality.

2. Positive Affirmations: Repeating positive affirmations can reprogram the subconscious mind to adopt new beliefs and habits. Speak or write them down and repeat them every day.

3. Meditation: Meditation is an excellent tool to reach the subconscious mind. By stilling the mind and focusing on your breath, you can connect with the subconscious mind and make positive changes.

4. Creative Visualization: Create a vision board with pictures that represent your goals and desires. Place it in a prominent place where you will see it often. Your subconscious mind will be reminded of what you want to achieve.

5. Auto-Suggestion: This technique involves repeating a positive statement to yourself every day. Your subconscious mind will eventually accept the statement as true and work to make it a reality.

6. Hypnosis: Hypnosis is a powerful tool to access the subconscious mind. A qualified hypnotherapist can guide you into a relaxed state and suggest new beliefs and behaviors to your subconscious mind.

7. Writing: Writing down your goals and desires can help you connect with your subconscious mind. The act of writing engages the subconscious mind, making it more receptive to change.

8. Brainwave Entrainment: This technique involves listening to sounds or music that have been designed to entrain the brain to specific frequencies. This can help you reach a deeper state of relaxation, making it easier to access the subconscious mind.

9. Lucid Dreaming: During lucid dreaming, you become aware that you are dreaming and can control the dream. This can be used to visualize your goals and connect with your subconscious mind.

10. Yoga: Yoga is an excellent way to connect with your subconscious mind. The practice involves focusing on your breath and body, which can help you reach a deeper state of relaxation and connect with your inner self.

Reflect on what you've learned in this chapter and identify practical ways to put it into action.

CHAPTER SIXTEEN

Anger Signature

Anger and Hatred

It's important to understand that anger and hatred can never solve a conflict. They only create more problems and make the situation worse. As the Buddhist saying goes, "Hatred is never appeased by hatred in this world. By non-hatred alone is hatred appeased." Even the Buddha himself experienced discrimination and suffering, but he never resorted to hatred or violence to overcome it. Instead, he chose the path of compassion and understanding.

In any conflict, choosing compassion and non-violence is the best way to protect yourself and others from further harm. This doesn't mean that you have to let yourself be bullied or abused. You can still protect yourself, but by doing so in a non-violent manner. For example, when faced with bullying, you can empower yourself by reminding yourself of your own goodness and the fact that their insults cannot hurt you. You can also try to understand the root cause of the bullying and extend compassion to the person who is bullying you.

One practical solution is to take deep breaths and count from 1 to 100 to calm yourself down. You can also walk away from the situation if possible, or try to diffuse the situation with humor. If the bullying becomes serious, you may need to seek help from authorities or others who can provide support and protection.

Ultimately, by focusing on your own giftedness and inner strength, you can see that you are more than what others say about you. By choosing compassion and non-violence, you can break the cycle of hatred and violence and help create a more peaceful and harmonious world.

Subtle Things of Life- learning from upanishads

The Upanishads, ancient Hindu scriptures, hold valuable lessons on how to live a harmonious life filled with inner peace and happiness. One such lesson is the importance of compassion and non-hatred. The Brihadaranyaka Upanishad states, "As a man who has found a treasure of wealth, you have found yourself. Guard yourself well, for a treasure like this is hard to find." This is a reminder that our inner wealth and self-worth is not determined by external circumstances or people. We should guard our inner peace and happiness and not let negative thoughts or actions of others affect us.

Another Upanishad, the Mandukya Upanishad, says "Om is the universe, and this is the exposition of Om. The past, the present, and the future, all that was, all that is, all that will be, is Om." This verse highlights the unity of all things and the interconnectedness of the universe. When we understand this, we realize that everyone and everything is connected and that our actions have a ripple effect. By choosing compassion and non-hatred, we are not only helping ourselves, but we are also creating a positive impact on the world around us.

The Katha Upanishad also touches on the importance of self-reflection and self-improvement. It states, "One who has no peace, and who is not satisfied within himself, how can he find peace anywhere?" When we are not at peace with ourselves, we cannot find peace in the world. Therefore, it is important to take the time to reflect on our own thoughts and actions and make improvements where necessary. By doing so, we can live a life filled with inner peace and happiness.

In conclusion, the lessons from the Upanishads emphasize the importance of compassion, non-hatred, self-reflection, and self-improvement. By incorporating these teachings into our lives, we can live a harmonious life filled with inner peace and happiness.

Anger is a destructive emotion

"Anger is a destructive emotion that not only hurts others, but also destroys the person experiencing it. It is a result of a strong identification with certain beliefs and ways of living, which leads to an exclusion of others who do not align with those beliefs. This exclusion leads to anger, which can result in irrational and harmful actions.

The price of anger is not worth the reward, as it leaves lasting scars and wounds, much like hammering nails into a fence. The more we hold onto our anger, the more we exclude and separate ourselves from the rest of existence, leading to a feeling of being trapped.

The root cause of anger is ignorance of ourselves, as we seek intensity in life. Instead of resorting to anger as a means of release, it is important to be aware of when we are feeling angry and to seek liberation through inclusion, rather than exclusion. By becoming aware of our own emotions and understanding ourselves, we can break free from the chains of anger and live a peaceful and harmonious life."

Be aware of your mortality

The Upanishads, ancient Indian texts that form the foundation of Hindu philosophy, offer a different perspective on mortality. They emphasize that the true nature of the self is immortal and unchanging, and that death is simply a release from the physical body. According to the Upanishads, the individual soul (Atman) is a spark of the divine, infinite consciousness (Brahman) that pervades the universe. When a person realizes the true nature of their self as being one with Brahman, they are no longer afraid of death.

In the words of the Upanishads, "As a person sheds worn-out clothes and puts on new ones, the soul discards worn-out bodies and wears new ones" (Bhagavad Gita 2.22). Death is seen as a necessary process for the soul to continue its journey and attain ultimate liberation (moksha).

By recognizing our mortality, we can begin to live each moment to the fullest, focusing on our relationships with others and on our own personal growth and development. This awareness of our own mortality can lead to a more meaningful and fulfilling life, as we make the most of every day and strive to live in accordance with our values and beliefs.

The Upanishads offer a unique perspective on mortality, emphasizing that the true self is immortal and that death is a necessary process for spiritual growth and liberation. By being aware of our mortality, we can live our lives with purpose and meaning, making the most of every moment and focusing on what truly matters.

The idea of living each day like it's your last is a powerful one, as it encourages us to focus on what truly matters and to live our lives with purpose and intention. By embracing this mindset, we can break free from the distractions and worries of everyday life and truly focus on the present moment.

In the Upanishads, this idea is emphasized through the concept of impermanence and the understanding that life is fleeting. By recognizing that our time on earth is limited, we can appreciate the present moment and make the most of our time here.

This is why it is important to live with a sense of urgency, to pursue our passions, to make amends with those we have hurt, and to cultivate a deep sense of gratitude for every moment we have. When we live in this way, we find a sense of peace and contentment that is not easily disturbed by the ups and downs of life.

Living each day like it's your last can be a transformative experience that brings new meaning and purpose to our lives. It helps us to live mindfully, to be present in every moment, and to pursue our goals with a sense of purpose and intention.

Own awareness

It is important to be in control of your, own awareness as it affects the way you live your life and the experiences you have. Being aware of your thoughts, emotions, and actions can help you to live in the present moment and avoid getting caught up in distractions. When you control your awareness, you are able to direct your energy towards what is important to you, and create a life that aligns with your values and goals. By practicing mindfulness and focusing your attention on the present moment, you can develop greater awareness and control over your thoughts and emotions, leading to a more fulfilling and meaningful life. So, take control of your awareness, be mindful of the present moment, and live a life that is fulfilling and meaningful.

Concentration

Concentration is a valuable skill that can bring many benefits to our daily lives. It involves keeping our awareness focused on one thing for an extended period of time. This allows us to be more present in our interactions with others, and to be more productive and efficient in our tasks. To get better at concentration, it is important to practice it in our daily lives, not just in a ten-minute meditation session. This means integrating it into everything we do, from speaking with others to doing our work. By giving our full attention to the task at hand, we can become more observant and able to solve problems more quickly. It also creates a powerful feeling when others can feel our concentration and focus on them, making our interactions more meaningful and effective.

Kindness Act

kindness not only helps the receiver, but it also has a profound impact on the giver. Kindness has been scientifically proven to increase happiness and decrease stress levels. It triggers the release of endorphins, which are natural painkillers and mood boosters, creating a positive and happy cycle of kindness. When we perform an act of kindness, it also fosters a sense of connection and belonging, reminding us that we are part of something larger and meaningful.

Acts of kindness can be simple and small, yet still have a big impact on the world. Holding the door open for someone, smiling at a stranger, listening to a friend in need, and donating blood are just a few examples of acts of kindness that can make a difference.

Moreover, practicing kindness on a daily basis helps to build a more compassionate and empathetic society. When we are kind to others, we are also showing others that it's okay to be kind. This creates a ripple effect, where acts of kindness can spread from person to person, making the world a better place.

Life is a precious gift, and we should strive to make the most of it. Being kind to others not only helps them, but it also makes us feel better about ourselves and contributes to creating a happier and more harmonious world. Let's strive to be a little kinder today, and make the world a better place for everyone.

What new perspectives or ideas have you gained from this chapter? Write 3 Points

• 86 •

CHAPTER SEVENTEEN

Quality Over Quantity Signature

Quality Over Quantity Signature

"Quality over Quantity" is a phrase that emphasizes the importance of having a few meaningful relationships, rather than a large number of superficial ones. In my life, I've learned that the people you surround yourself with have a profound impact on your well-being, both mentally and emotionally. That's why it's so important to choose friends who bring positivity, support, and growth into your life, rather than those who bring negativity, drama, and distractions.

Just like in the epic tale of Ramayana, where Lord Rama chose a small group of loyal companions, Hanuman and Lakshman, to help him on his journey to defeat the demon king Ravana. Although Lord Rama was offered a large army to accompany him, he chose to rely on a few trustworthy allies, who were dedicated to his cause and helped him achieve his goal.

Similarly, in our lives, it's better to have a few close friends who are there for us, rather than a large group of acquaintances who may not be there in our time of need. Quality over Quantity applies not only to our friendships but to all aspects of our life, from the food we eat to the clothes we wear, it's essential to prioritize quality over quantity.

I've learned that having a few close friends, who understand us and support us, can bring more joy and fulfillment into our lives than a large number of superficial relationships. So let's make an effort to choose friends for quality over quantity, and cultivate meaningful relationships that enrich our lives.

"True friendship is the cornerstone of a virtuous life." As the Buddha once said, "When a monk has admirable friends, companions, and comrades, he can be expected to develop and pursue the noble eightfold path." It's better to choose quality over quantity when it comes to the people we surround ourselves with. Our life's journey is not a solitary one, and along the way, we meet many people. However, not everyone we encounter is a positive influence on our lives. Negative peer pressure can lead to the adoption of bad habits. It's easy to find friends when we are wealthy, famous, or prosperous, but it's in our times of need when true friends reveal themselves.

As William Arthur Ward said, "The mediocre teacher tells. The good teacher explains. The superior teacher demonstrates. The great teacher inspires." In the same way, good friends are those who inspire us to greatness, who encourage us to be our best selves and to make virtuous choices. On the other hand, bad friends can lead us astray, push us towards vices, and hinder our personal growth. As the saying goes, "Birds of a feather flock together." So, let's choose to flock with those who will bring out the best in us.

Distance yourself from someone who has a negative impact

"How can you distance yourself from someone who has a negative impact on you and triggers stress and unhappiness? Consider these practical tips:

1. Dedicate a few minutes each day to reflect on the harm that stressful individuals have on you.
2. Analyze the impact of their words and emotions on your mental and emotional state, as well as your behavior. If you are unsatisfied with the situation, take action.
3. Visualize yourself staying calm and composed, unaffected by the stress, anxiety, and strain they bring.
4. Develop a plan to minimize their influence on you, such as avoiding them, ignoring their words, or changing the subject.
5. During stressful situations, practice deep breathing and hydrate if possible.

What is important?

Rather than a larger quantity of something that is of lower quality. This idea can be applied to many aspects of life, including our possessions, our relationships, and even our time.

When it comes to possessions, it can be easy to fall into the trap of accumulating more and more things in the pursuit of happiness. However, studies have shown that beyond a certain point, having more material possessions does not lead to increased happiness or life satisfaction. Instead, we may find greater happiness by focusing on owning fewer, higher quality possessions that we truly value and appreciate.

In relationships, quality over quantity means prioritizing deep, meaningful connections with a few close friends or family members, rather than trying to maintain many superficial relationships. By investing time and energy into cultivating these meaningful connections, we can build a strong support network that brings us greater happiness and fulfillment.

When it comes to our time, quality over quantity means prioritizing activities and experiences that bring us joy and contribute to our overall well-being, rather than simply trying to pack as much into our schedules as possible. This might mean saying "no" to certain commitments, or making time for self-care activities like exercise, meditation, or spending time in nature.

In today's fast-paced world, it can be easy to get caught up in the idea that more is always better. However, by prioritizing quality over quantity, we can live more intentional, fulfilling lives that align with our values and bring us greater happiness and satisfaction.

Based on this chapter, what changes do you plan to make in your life going forward?

CHAPTER EIGHTEEN

Gratitude Signature

The Power of Gratitude

The concept of gratitude is a powerful tool that can bring about significant positive changes in our lives. It is an attitude of appreciation and thankfulness towards the people, situations, and things in our lives. Science has proven that cultivating a gratitude mindset can improve our mental and physical health, increase productivity, and enhance our relationships. Gratitude doesn't require any monetary investment, and it is easy to practice.

When we cultivate an attitude of gratitude, we attract what we want. This is known as the law of attraction. The law of attraction states that we attract into our lives the things we focus on. So, when we focus on things we are thankful for, we attract more of those things into our lives. For example, if we are grateful for having a supportive partner, we will attract more supportive people into our lives.

Gratitude is also instrumental in improving relationships. Saying "thank you" is a fundamental lesson we learn as children, and it is a powerful tool to build and maintain healthy relationships. When we appreciate the people in our lives, we positively impact our relationship with them. For instance, if we are thankful for our colleagues, we are more likely to have better communication and teamwork.

Gratitude reduces negativity in our lives. It is hard to be negative when we focus on things we are thankful for. When we count our blessings, we improve our mood and outlook. For example, if we are grateful for our health, we are less likely to focus on our illness and more likely to feel positive about our overall well-being.

Cultivating gratitude also enhances problem-solving skills. When we focus on gratitude, we open our minds to new possibilities and connections. It helps us approach problems from a positive perspective, with a mindset of improvement and opportunity. For example, if we are grateful for our job, we are more likely to approach workplace challenges with a positive mindset, and find creative solutions to problems.

Gratitude also helps us learn and grow. Every problem has an opportunity for growth and learning. Being grateful for the opportunities to learn new things can help us stay motivated, even when things get tough. For example, if we are grateful for the opportunity to learn a new skill, we are more likely to stick with it and achieve our goals.

Gratitude is a powerful tool that can bring about significant positive changes in our lives. It can improve our mental and physical health, increase productivity, and enhance our relationships. The best part about gratitude is that it requires no monetary investment and is easy to practice. So, let's make gratitude a habit in our daily lives and watch as it transforms us and the world around us.

21 reasons to practice the gratidude

1. Gratitude attracts what we want: By focusing on what we are grateful for, we can attract more of those things into our lives. The more we express gratitude for the good things in our lives, the more positive things we will attract.

2. Gratitude improves relationships: Expressing gratitude towards the people in our lives can strengthen our relationships with them. When we appreciate someone's contributions and talents, they feel valued and recognized, leading to a more positive and supportive relationship.

3. Gratitude reduces negativity: When we focus on the positive aspects of our lives and express gratitude for them, it becomes difficult to dwell on negative thoughts and emotions. Gratitude can help shift our focus from what's going wrong to what's going right, leading to a more positive outlook.

4. Gratitude improves problem-solving skills: Expressing gratitude can help us approach problems with a more positive mindset. Instead of seeing problems as insurmountable barriers, we can see them as opportunities for growth and improvement.

5. Gratitude helps us learn: By expressing gratitude for our experiences, even the difficult ones, we can find the silver lining and focus on the lessons we can learn. Gratitude can help us see challenges as opportunities for personal growth and development.

6. Gratitude promotes mindfulness: When we are grateful, we are fully present in the moment and appreciate what we have. Practicing gratitude regularly can help us become more mindful and grounded.

7. Gratitude improves sleep: Expressing gratitude before bedtime can lead to a more peaceful and restful sleep. Gratitude can help calm the mind and reduce stress and anxiety, leading to better sleep quality.

8. Gratitude boosts self-esteem: By expressing gratitude for our own accomplishments and strengths, we can boost our self-esteem and feel more confident in ourselves.

9. Gratitude improves mental health: Regularly expressing gratitude has been linked to improved mental health, including reduced symptoms of depression and anxiety.

10. Gratitude reduces materialism: Focusing on what we are grateful for can help us appreciate what we already have and reduce the

desire for material possessions.

11. Gratitude promotes resilience: When we express gratitude during difficult times, we can develop a sense of resilience and the ability to overcome challenges.

12. Gratitude strengthens emotional intelligence: Expressing gratitude can help us become more aware of our own emotions and the emotions of others, leading to stronger emotional intelligence.

13. Gratitude improves physical health: Studies have shown that expressing gratitude can lead to improved physical health, including lower blood pressure and a stronger immune system.

14. Gratitude fosters forgiveness: When we express gratitude towards those who have wronged us, it can help us let go of negative emotions and foster forgiveness.

15. Gratitude encourages prosocial behavior: Expressing gratitude towards others can inspire them to be more prosocial and helpful to others.

16. Gratitude improves decision-making: By approaching decisions with a mindset of gratitude, we can make more thoughtful and positive choices.

17. Gratitude enhances creativity: Focusing on the positive aspects of our experiences can help us see new possibilities and come up with more creative ideas.

18. Gratitude promotes altruism: Expressing gratitude can inspire us to be more altruistic and do good for others.

19. Gratitude strengthens social connections: By expressing gratitude towards others, we can strengthen our social connections and feel a greater sense of belonging.

20. Gratitude increases happiness: Studies have shown that regularly practicing gratitude can lead to increased levels of happiness and life satisfaction.

21. Gratitude is contagious: When we express gratitude towards others, it can inspire them to do the same and create a ripple effect of positivity and gratitude.

15 tips for practicing gratitude every day

1. Start your day with gratitude: Before you even get out of bed, think about three things you're grateful for. This can set the tone for the rest of the day.
2. Keep a gratitude journal: Write down three to five things you're grateful for each day. This helps you focus on the positive aspects of your life.
3. Express gratitude to others: Let people know that you appreciate them. This can be as simple as saying "thank you" or writing a note of appreciation.
4. Practice mindfulness: Be present in the moment and focus on what you're grateful for. Take time to appreciate the little things in life.
5. Use visual reminders: Place reminders of things you're grateful for in places you'll see them often, like post-it notes on your mirror or a photo on your desk.
6. Practice gratitude during meals: Take a moment before eating to appreciate the food, the people you're sharing the meal with, and any other positive aspects of the meal.
7. Think of others: Take time to think of people who have helped you or made a positive impact in your life. Be grateful for them.
8. Turn negative thoughts into positive ones: When negative thoughts arise, consciously try to reframe them in a positive way.
9. Meditate on gratitude: Take a few minutes each day to meditate on gratitude. Visualize the things you're grateful for and let yourself feel the positive emotions associated with them.
10. Take a gratitude walk: Go for a walk and think about everything you're grateful for. Being in nature can amplify the positive emotions associated with gratitude.

11. Practice gratitude in challenging situations: When faced with a difficult situation, try to find something positive to focus on. This can help you feel more grounded and less stressed.

12. Practice gratitude before bed: Take a few minutes before bed to reflect on the positive things that happened during the day. This can help you fall asleep feeling more content.

13. Volunteer or help others: Helping others can increase feelings of gratitude and purpose.

14. Surround yourself with positivity: Spend time with people who uplift you and focus on positive news and media.

15. Practice gratitude every day: Make gratitude a daily habit. The more you practice, the more natural it will become.

By implementing these tips, you can cultivate a daily practice of gratitude that can lead to a more positive outlook on life, increased happiness, and improved relationships with others.

Describe how the insights from this chapter will impact your mindset and actions.

CHAPTER NINETEEN

Learning Signature

If you fall down 100 times, under lessons to be learnt.

Life is a precious gift that should be cherished and lived to the fullest. It is a journey that should bring joy, happiness, and fulfillment. Unfortunately, not everyone lives their lives in this way. For some, life can seem unfulfilling and dull. But it is important to remember that you have the power to change this. If you are not living a life that brings you joy, it is time to make some changes.

To live a joyful life, you first need to know what you want. This may seem like a simple task, but it is often the hardest part of the journey. To get to know yourself, you need to understand your mind and learn how to manage your energy wisely. This is essential in creating a life that is truly fulfilling.

One key aspect of this journey is committing to your goals. When you fall down 100 times in a day, it may seem like failure, but for a committed individual, it is simply a lesson to be learned. When you are committed to your goals, your mind becomes organized, and this will have a ripple effect on the rest of your life. The way you think influences the way you feel, and your emotions become organized. When your thought, emotions, and energy are all organized in the same direction, your body will follow suit. This alignment will allow you to create and manifest what you truly desire in life.

It is important to remember that you are the creator of your own life. The source of creation is within you, always present in every moment. By focusing on what you want and managing your energy wisely, you can create a life that is filled with joy, happiness, and fulfillment. So don't be afraid to take the reins of your life and create the world you truly want to live in. Life is meant to be lived joyfully, and it is up to you to make it so.

The key to living a joyful life is to know what you want and align your thoughts, emotions, energy, and actions towards that goal. This takes self-awareness, discipline, and a strong commitment to creating a life that brings you happiness and fulfillment.

One of the most important aspects of creating a joyful life is learning how to manage your energy. Energy is the currency of life and it's essential to invest it wisely. This means prioritizing the things that bring you joy and fulfillment and avoiding those that drain you. For example, spending time with positive people who support and encourage you will bring you energy, while spending time with negative people will drain you.

Another important aspect of creating a joyful life is to understand your thoughts and emotions. Your thoughts and emotions are powerful forces that shape your reality. If you focus on positive and empowering thoughts, you will experience a positive and joyful life. On the other hand, if you focus on negative and disempowering thoughts, you will experience a negative and unhappy life. It's important to be mindful of your thoughts and emotions and to take control of them, rather than allowing them to control you.

To live a joyful life, you must also be committed to taking action towards your goals. This means taking steps each day to bring you closer to your desired reality. It's important to remember that action is not just physical movement, but also mental and emotional effort. For example, taking the time to meditate and focus on positive thoughts is an important form of action that contributes to your overall well-being and happiness.

Ultimately, living a joyful life is about taking control of your mind, emotions, energy, and actions, and aligning them towards your goals and desires. This requires effort and commitment, but the reward of a happy and fulfilling life is well worth it. Remember, you are the creator of your life, so create it in a way that brings you joy and happiness every day.

As the saying goes, "if you fall down 100 times, get up 101 times." The truth is, failure is a natural part of life, and we all experience setbacks and obstacles along the way. However, it is often in these moments of failure that we have the opportunity to learn and grow the most.

One real-life example of this is the story of J.K. Rowling. Before she became the best-selling author of the Harry Potter series, Rowling faced a series of setbacks and failures. She was rejected by multiple publishers before finally being accepted, and at one point, she was even homeless and living on welfare. However, despite these challenges, Rowling continued to persevere and pursue her passion for writing. In doing so, she not only achieved her own dreams, but also inspired millions of readers around the world.

Another example is the story of Michael Jordan. Widely regarded as one of the greatest basketball players of all time, Jordan faced numerous failures and setbacks throughout his career. He was cut from his high school basketball team, and later faced defeats in the NBA Finals. However, rather than giving up, Jordan used these setbacks as motivation to work even harder and become a better player. His perseverance and determination helped him achieve his goals and become a legend in his sport.

These examples demonstrate the importance of persistence and resilience in the face of failure. While setbacks and obstacles may be discouraging, they also present an opportunity to learn and grow. By reflecting on our failures and identifying the lessons to be learned, we can move forward with greater knowledge and understanding. In this way, we can turn our failures into opportunities for growth and ultimately, achieve greater success in our lives.

Based on your understanding of this chapter, how will you approach situations differently in the future?

CHAPTER TWENTY

Forgiveness Signature

Forgive others and yourself

Forgive others and yourself Forgive others and yourself for any past mistakes or hurtful actions. Holding grudges and harboring resentment will only cause you more pain in the long run. Practice forgiveness and let go of any negative feelings towards others and towards yourself. This will not only bring peace to your life but also to the lives of those around you.

Practice gratitude Practice gratitude and focus on the positive aspects of your life and the good things that people have done for you. By focusing on the positive, you will be able to develop a more optimistic outlook on life and find more happiness in your relationships with others.

Communicate openly and honestly Communicate openly and honestly with others. When conflicts arise, it's important to express your thoughts and feelings in a calm and respectful manner. By doing so, you can work towards resolving the issue and finding a mutually beneficial solution.

Focus on solutions, not problems Instead of dwelling on the problems and negative aspects of a situation, focus on finding solutions. By shifting your focus to finding solutions, you will be able to find peace and happiness in even the most challenging of circumstances.

Develop healthy relationships Develop healthy relationships with others. Surround yourself with positive and supportive people who will lift you up and help you to find peace and happiness in life. Avoid toxic relationships that bring negativity and drama into your life.

What is forgiveness

Forgiveness is a complex and multi-faceted concept that is deeply rooted in human emotions and relationships. At its core, forgiveness is the act of letting go of negative feelings and emotions towards someone who has caused us harm. It is a process of releasing anger, bitterness, resentment and other negative emotions that can hold us back from moving forward and finding peace and happiness in our lives.

Forgiveness is not just about the person who has been wronged, but it is also about the person who has done the wrong. By forgiving, we can free ourselves from the burden of negative emotions and find peace and happiness, and we can also help the person who has done us wrong to heal and move forward.

Why to forgive?

There are many reasons why we should forgive, including:

1. Improved mental and physical health: Holding onto anger and bitterness can take a toll on our mental and physical health. Forgiveness can help reduce stress, lower blood pressure, and improve overall well-being.
2. Improved relationships: Forgiveness can help improve our relationships with others, allowing us to rebuild trust and create

stronger bonds with those we have forgiven.

3. Personal growth: Forgiveness is a powerful tool for personal growth and self-discovery. By letting go of negative emotions and forgiving those who have hurt us, we can gain insight into our own behavior and emotions and grow as individuals.

4. Finding peace: Forgiveness can help us find peace in our lives and move forward from the past, allowing us to focus on the present and the future.

How to forgive

However, forgiving is not always easy. It can be difficult to let go of negative feelings and emotions, especially if the harm that was done was severe. It is important to understand that forgiveness is not forgetting, nor is it excusing the behavior of the person who has caused harm. Instead, it is about recognizing the harm that was done and choosing to let go of the negative emotions associated with it.

So, how do we forgive? The process of forgiveness is different for everyone, but here are some steps that can help:

1. Acknowledge the harm: The first step in forgiving is to acknowledge the harm that was done. This means recognizing and accepting the pain and emotions that we are feeling.

2. Let go of anger and bitterness: Once we have acknowledged the harm, we can begin to let go of our anger and bitterness. This can be done by practicing mindfulness and focusing on our breath and the present moment.

3. Empathize with the person who caused harm: It can be helpful to try to understand why the person who caused harm did what they did. This does not excuse their behavior, but it can help us to understand their motivations and let go of our anger and

bitterness.

4. Make a conscious choice to forgive: Forgiveness is a conscious choice, and it is important to make that choice with intention. This can be done by repeating affirmations, visualizing the process of forgiving, or writing a letter of forgiveness.

5. Practice forgiveness: Forgiveness is not a one-time event, but a process that takes time and effort. It is important to practice forgiveness daily by letting go of negative emotions and focusing on love, compassion and peace.

When to forgive?

When is the right time to forgive? There is no one answer to this question, as everyone's process is different. Some people may be able to forgive quickly, while others may need more time. It is important to listen to your own heart and emotions and forgive when you are ready. But I am sure we are never ready. So NOW is the right time to forigve.

Whom to forgive?

Forgiving others who have caused us harm is an important aspect of the forgiveness process. This can be someone who has physically, emotionally, or verbally hurt us, or someone who has betrayed our trust or broken a promise. Holding onto grudges and resentment only leads to further negativity and suffering, and can prevent us from moving forward in life. Forgiveness, on the other hand, allows us to release these negative feelings and heal from the hurt.

Forgiving others can be difficult, especially if the harm they caused us was significant. However, it is important to understand that forgiving someone does not mean condoning their behavior or forgetting what happened. Rather, it is about letting go of the resentment and anger that we hold towards them, and finding a way to peacefully coexist with them, even if there is no relationship between us.

Forgiveness can also be applied to oneself. Self-forgiveness is about accepting and letting go of past mistakes, wrongdoings, and negative self-talk. It is about treating oneself with kindness and compassion, instead of being overly critical or harsh. Self-forgiveness is an essential part of personal growth and can help us to feel more confident and self-assured.

In the Hindu epic, the Mahabharata, the theme of forgiveness is exemplified in the character of Bhishma. Bhishma, a warrior prince, takes a vow of celibacy in order to serve his father and kingdom. Despite the suffering he faces as a result of his vow, he continues to serve his kingdom selflessly and with devotion. In a battle, Bhishma is struck down by an arrow, but refuses to die until he receives the forgiveness of his enemies, the Pandavas. When Yudhishthira, the king of the Pandavas, visits Bhishma on his deathbed, Bhishma asks for his forgiveness. Yudhishthira, being a man of dharma, forgives Bhishma and blesses him to die peacefully.

Similarly, we too can learn the importance of seeking and granting forgiveness. When we forgive others, we release the negative emotions that are holding us back, and allow ourselves to move forward. When we forgive ourselves, we let go of self-criticism and guilt, and allow ourselves to grow and thrive.

Forgiveness is an important aspect of personal growth and happiness. Whether it is forgiving others who have caused us harm or forgiving ourselves for past mistakes, the act of forgiveness allows us to release negative emotions, heal from hurt, and move forward with a positive and peaceful outlook on life.

What are some concrete steps you can take to build on the insights from this chapter? Whom do you forgive write 3 names

CHAPTER TWENTY-ONE

Happiness Signature

Happiness is inside !

1. When faced with disappointment, shift your focus to the positive and look for opportunities. This can help you see that there are other things that can bring you joy and happiness. It's a matter of being open to different experiences and letting go of attachments to specific outcomes.
2. Embrace flexibility and be open to new experiences. Sometimes, the unexpected can lead to something even better than what you originally had in mind. Being willing to try new things and adapt to changing circumstances can help you maintain a positive outlook.
3. Practice gratitude and appreciation for what you have. Instead of focusing on what you lost or what went wrong, focus on what you have and what you can be grateful for. You can still enjoy the food and wine, and the experience of having company even if it's not the original group you were expecting.
4. Stay present and mindful. Instead of letting frustration or impatience take over, try to stay in the present moment and be mindful of your surroundings. You might find that there are things to appreciate or enjoy even in mundane moments.
5. Practice emotional intelligence and self-control. When faced with difficult people or situations, don't let your emotions take

control. Instead, practice empathy and try to understand where the other person is coming from. You can choose to respond with kindness, compassion, or simply not engage.

6. Cultivate a positive mindset by focusing on the good in your life. This can help you build resilience and cope with challenges more effectively. Instead of dwelling on negative thoughts, focus on positive ones and look for opportunities to create more positive experiences in your life.

7. Keep a gratitude journal and write down things that you are thankful for each day. This can help you stay focused on the positive and cultivate a sense of gratitude in your life.

8. Surround yourself with positive people who uplift and inspire you. This can help you stay motivated and optimistic, and can also provide support when you face challenges.

9. Practice mindfulness meditation to help you stay centered and calm in the midst of stress or difficulty. This can also help you cultivate a sense of gratitude and appreciation for life.

10. Take care of your physical health by eating well, exercising regularly, and getting enough rest. This can help you maintain a positive outlook and feel good in your body.

11. Learn to let go of things that are outside of your control. This can help you stay focused on what you can do to improve your life and let go of negative emotions that can hold you back.

12. Practice forgiveness and compassion, both towards yourself and others. This can help you let go of grudges or negative feelings, and also cultivate a more positive outlook on life.

13. Take time to do things that you enjoy and that bring you happiness, whether it's spending time with loved ones, pursuing a hobby, or taking a relaxing bath. This can help you recharge and stay positive.

14. Stay curious and open-minded. This can help you learn and grow, and also stay engaged with the world around you.

15. Practice self-care and self-compassion. This can help you stay grounded and take care of yourself in difficult times, and also cultivate a sense of appreciation and gratitude for your own

strengths and abilities.

The characters in Mahabharata demonstrated happiness inspite of struggle in life

1. Bhishma: Bhishma, the wise and noble patriarch of the Kuru family, chose to remain happy and content despite being bound to a bed of arrows for many years. He found joy in sharing his wisdom and teachings with the young princes, and in his love for the divine.

2. Yudhishthira: Yudhishthira, the eldest of the Pandava brothers, demonstrated his happiness every day by remaining steadfast in his principles of righteousness and dharma, even in the face of great adversity. He found joy in doing his duty and serving his people, and in his unwavering faith in the divine.

3. Arjuna: Arjuna, the skilled warrior and archer, found happiness every day in his devotion to Lord Krishna and in his love for his brothers and his people. Despite facing many challenges and trials in his life, he remained focused on his goal and found joy in the service of others.

4. Draupadi: Draupadi, the noble and strong-willed wife of the Pandava brothers, demonstrated her happiness every day by remaining resilient and resourceful in the face of many difficulties and injustices. She found joy in her love for her husbands and her faith in the divine, and in her determination to overcome all obstacles.

5. Karna: Karna, the valiant warrior and loyal friend of Duryodhana, found happiness every day in his devotion to his friend and his sense of duty towards his family and his people. Despite facing many challenges and betrayals in his life, he remained steadfast in his principles and found joy in his love for

his mother and his unwavering faith in the divine.

One important factor in finding happiness is cultivating a sense of gratitude. This means focusing on the good things in our lives, rather than dwelling on the negative. Real-life examples of this can be seen in the practice of gratitude journaling, where individuals write down things they are grateful for each day, or in the act of expressing appreciation to others, whether through a thank-you note or a simple gesture of kindness.

Another key strategy for finding happiness is prioritizing meaningful relationships. Studies have shown that social connections are crucial to our well-being, and that having strong, supportive relationships can bring us greater happiness and a sense of belonging. Real-life examples of this can be seen in the way people prioritize spending time with loved ones, or in the effort they put into building and maintaining friendships.

Another strategy for finding happiness is pursuing activities and experiences that bring us joy and fulfillment. This might mean pursuing hobbies or interests that we are passionate about, or seeking out new experiences that challenge and inspire us. Real-life examples of this can be seen in the way people prioritize travel, or in the way they devote time and energy to creative pursuits like writing, painting, or music.

Finally, finding happiness often involves a shift in mindset, from a focus on external circumstances to an emphasis on internal well-being. This means prioritizing self-care activities like exercise, meditation, or spending time in nature, and learning to cultivate a sense of peace and contentment within ourselves. Real-life examples of this can be seen in the way people prioritize self-care, or in the way they seek out opportunities for personal growth and self-improvement.

In conclusion, finding happiness in life is a journey that requires effort and intentionality. By cultivating gratitude, prioritizing meaningful relationships, pursuing joy and fulfillment, and shifting our mindset towards internal well-being, we can all take steps towards greater happiness and fulfillment in our lives.

Describe the most important lesson you learned from this chapter and how you plan to incorporate it into your life.

Our Memories

ಾಪುದೇ ಕೆಲಸ ಮಾಡಿದ್ರೂ ಆದು ಕೈಗೂ
free telegram group.
k is in the description
JOIN OUR NEXT MASTER CLASS
R MORE INFORMATION CLICK ON DISCRIPTION
ಅರಮನೆಗೆ ದಸರಾ ಗಜಪಡೆಯ
description
15 ಮಂದಿ ಸೋಂಕಿತರಿಗೆ ಬಿಯಲಲ್ಲಿ ಚಿಕಿತ್ಸೆ
RIBE OUR CHANNEL FOR MORE HEALING TECHNIQUES
ೀವು ಯಾವುದೇ ಕೆಲಸ ಮಾಡಿದ್ರೂ ಆದು ಕೈಗೂಡುತ್ತಿಲ್ವಾ..?
 NEWS 1
vikalpa
Holistic
Centre
ಯ ಮನಸ್ಸು
JOIN OUR NEXT MASTER CLASS
Link in Description
LIV
ಸ್ಯಸೂರು ಅರಮನೆಗೆ ದಸರಾ ಗಜಪಡೆಯ 2ನೇ ತಂಡ ಆಗಮ
ಾದಿಗಾರರು:-ಚಕ್ರಪಾಣಿ-9880579202, ನಾಗಮಂಗಲ:-ಶ್ರೀನಿವಾ
06:34

Connect With Us

Since you bought this book, You will get 1-2-1 FREE consultation session for 30 Mins based on availability of slots

Savikalpa Holistic Center

Mobile 6364895551/9538735551
Youtube @savikalpaholisticcenter
Facebook Savikalpaholisticcenter
Website www.savikalpaholisticcenter.com